AN AMERICAN JOURNEY

Kermit Frazier
&
John Leicht

BROADWAY PLAY PUBLISHING INC
New York
www.broadwayplaypublishing.com
info@broadwayplaypublishing.com

First edition: November 2012
Second edition: February 2013
I S B N: 978-0-88145-552-6
Book design: Marie Donovan
Page make-up: Adobe Indesign
Typeface: Palatino
Printed and bound in the U S A

ABOUT THE AUTHORS

Kermit Frazier has had 18 plays produced in New York and around the country at such theaters as the Milwaukee Repertory Theater, Asolo Theatre Company, Seattle Children's Theatre, First Stage Children's Theater, Baltimore Center Stage, the Philadelphia Drama Guild, the Ensemble Studio Theatre, and the New Federal Theatre. His plays include KERNEL OF SANITY, DINAH WASHINGTON IS DEAD, CLASS REUNION, SHADOWS AND ECHOES, INTERSTICES, LEGACIES, AN AMERICAN JOURNEY, DREAM KING, SACRED PLACES, LITTLE ROCK, and SMOLDERING FIRES. He has also written for such series as *Gullah Gullah Island* (co-producer and executive story editor), *The Cosby Mysteries, The Magic School Bus, The Misadventures of Maya and Miguel, The Wonder Pets,* and *All My Children.* He was a creator of and head writer for the popular children's mystery series, *Ghostwriter.* "Drive," the first chapter of his memoir, was published in *Callaloo.* Other articles, reviews, and short stories have appeared in such magazines and journals as *Green Mountains Review, The Chicago Review, American Theater, Black World, Essence,* and *The New York Times Book Review.* He teaches in the M F A Program in Creative Writing at Adelphi University.

John Leicht is a playwright and novelist now living in Raleigh, North Carolina. John was Playwright-In-Residence for the Milwaukee Repertory Theater from 1986-1995. His mainstage productions at the M R T were AN AMERICAN JOURNEY (with Kermit Frazier) and MOOT. Other notable plays are a stage adaptation of *Huckleberry Finn* and *The Irish Chord* (with Michael Neville) for First Stage Milwaukee; SEQUOYAH, THE TRAIL OF TEARS for the Cherokee Heritage Center, CAFÉ DES BON TEMPS (also with Michael Neville) for Playwrights Studio Theater, and a new play CIVILIZATION. John's novels are *Gardyloo!* and a work-in-progress, *Making the Music*. John, his wife Debra and their Golden Retriever, Chiller, live in a warm, cozy home set within the modest confines of their very own, little woods.

AN AMERICAN JOURNEY was first produced at the Milwaukee Repertory Theater (Managing Director, Sara O'Connor) from 16 January-22 February 1987. The cast and creative contributors were:

SYLVIA BELL WHITE	Tamu Gray
DOCK BELL	Lex Monson
DANIEL BELL	Larry G Malvern
PATRICK BELL	Emil Herrera
ERNEST BELL	Peter Jay Fernandez
JIMMY BELL	Larry G Malvern
DOUGLAS WHITE	Larry G Malvern
EMMA CLARK	Sylvia Carter
PATROLMAN THOMAS GRADY	Matthew A Loney
PATROLMAN LOUIS KRAUSE	Peter Silbert
D A WILLIAM MCCAULEY	Richard Riehle
MEDICAL EXAMINER JOSEPH LAMONTE	Kenneth Albers
DETECTIVE RUSSELL VORPAGEL	Daniel Mooney
WILLIAM HOCHSTAETTER	James Pickering
EUGENE BRADSHAW	Peter Jay Fernandez
ATTORNEY HAMILTON	Julian E Brown
CHARLES WILSON	Steven J Gefroh
PREACHER	Emil Herrera
CHIEF OF POLICE JOHNSON	Kenneth Albers
MAYOR ZEIDLER	James Pickering
TUCKER	Steven J. Gefroh
SOCIAL WORKER	Johanna Melamed
PLAINTIFF LAWYERS	J. Michael Brennan, Rose Pickering
DEFENSE LAWYERS	Kenneth Albers, Steven J Gefroh
PROSPECTIVE JURORS	Sylvia Carter, Johanna Melamed, Lex Monson, James Pickering

POLICE SERGEANT.................................... Robert Bennett, Jr.
MORGUE ATTENDANT... Ted Tyson
INSPECTOR GLASER...................................... Kenneth Albers
CAPTAIN WOELFEL .... James Pickering
JUDGE... J Michael Brennan
CROWD PEOPLE/WIRETAPPERS/PHOTOGRAPHERS/
REPORTERS/VOICES...
Robert Bennett Jr, J Michael Brennan, Julian E Brown,
Sylvia Carter, Sara Chazen, Peter Jay Fernandez, Larry
G Malvern, Johanna Melamed, Lex Monson, Ted Tyson

Director.. John Dillon
Set designers ....Laura Maurer, Tim Thomas
Production stage manager.........................Rob Goodman
Stage manager .... Diane Carlin-Bartel
Costume designer ....Carol Oditz
Lighting designer.................................... Victor En Yu Tan
Properties director ....Samuel A. Garst
Assistant costume designer .... Diane Dalton
Properties artisan .... Sandra J Strawn

CHARACTERS

SYLVIA BELL WHITE, *black woman, fifty-five*
DOCK BELL, *black man, late sixties*
DANIEL BELL, *black man, twenty-two*
PATRICK BELL, *black man, thirties to sixties*
ERNEST BELL, *black man, twenties to forties*
JIMMY BELL, *black man, twenties*
DOUGLAS WHITE, *black man, twenty*
EMMA CLARK, *black woman, mid-forties*
THOMAS GRADY, *white man, twenties to forties*
LOUIS KRAUSE, *white man, twenties to forties*
WILLIAM MCCAULEY, *white man, fifties*
JOSEPH LAMONTE, *white man, fifties*
RUSSELL VORPAGEL, *white man, late twenties to late forties*
WILLIAM HOCHSTAETTER, *white man, late fifties*
EUGENE BRADSHAW, *black man, mid-forties*
ATTORNEY HAMILTON, *black man, mid-forties*
REPORTER #1, *white man or woman*
REPORTER #2, *white man or woman*
CHARLES WILSON, *white man, middle aged*
BLACK PERSON #1, #2, #3,#4, #5
BLACK PREACHER, *man, thirties*
CHIEF JOHNSON, *white man, middle aged*
MAYOR ZEIDLER, *white man, middle aged*
TUCKER, *white man, middle-aged*
SOCIAL WORKER, *white woman, thirties*
PLAINTIFF LAWYER #1, *white, thirties*
PLAINTIFF LAWYER #2, *white, thirties*

DEFENSE LAWYER #1, *white, thirties*
DEFENSE LAWYER #2, *white, thirties*
PROSPECTIVE JURORS, *white man, white woman, black man, black woman*
POLICE SERGEANT, *white man, thirties*
MORGUE ATTENDANT, *white, late twenties*
INSPECTOR GLASER, *white man, middle aged*
CAPTAIN WOELFEL, *white man, middle aged*
JUDGE, *white man, sixties*
WIRETAP MEN (2), *white, thirties*

Note: *Some of the characters appear at more than one age in the course of the play. the Milwaukee Repertory Theater production involved the use of twenty actors: 5 black males, 2 black females, ten white males, three white females.*

SETTING

The times: The present and various times between 1936 and now.

The place: America

Staging and setting: A ramshackle and no longer functional, one room, black built schoolhouse. Circa 1910. US, a wall with an old, planked blackboard. Door. Wooden, planked floor. A chair and old school desk are overturned.

The schoolroom functions as a neutral space for all the locations and scenes of the play.

Particular attention should be given to lighting to foster clarity in terms of SYLVIA's many and rapid shifts of consciousness.

This play represents the authors' views after having researched the facts. There are times in the play when characters speak words supplied by the authors that are not necessarily the actual words in any existing document. However, the authors have based such dialogue on actual facts and events that are true.

ACT ONE

(SYLVIA *enters through schoolhouse door. She carries a large, shoulder-strapped satchel. She looks about the room, pats the blackboard, approaches the overturned desk and chair. She sets them aright during the first few moments of the play. Dusts off the desk. Sets down the satchel)*

SYLVIA: My grade school teacher's name was Mrs Emma Clark.

(MRS CLARK *appears.)*

SYLVIA: She taught me good. I always wondered who taught her.

(KRAUSE *and* GRADY *enter. Full motorcycle police uniform for both)*

KRAUSE: Tom?

GRADY: Yeah?

KRAUSE: You got a cigarette?

GRADY: Yeah. Here.

(GRADY *lights* KRAUSE's *cigarette.)*

SYLVIA: After I left this ol' grade school I had some other teachers. Mister Louis Krause and MisterThomas Grady. Two Milwaukee motorcycle policemen. I wonder who taught them.

KRAUSE: Seen any action tonight?

GRADY: Nothin'. Gonna get some arrests.

KRAUSE: Yeah.

GRADY: Figure I'd check out them vacant homes 'round Seventh, Eighth and Vine.

KRAUSE: Yeah.

GRADY: Arrest some niggers.

MRS CLARK: Sylvia?

SYLVIA: Taught me the best she could.

MRS CLARK: Sylvia. I want to talk to you about your education.

SYLVIA: She called me aside that last day.

MRS CLARK: You got natural ability. Good speller. Got yourself a lot of words for a girl your age. But don't stop just 'cause you graduatin'. More words you get, smarter you are. Be surprised what you know when all is said and done.

SYLVIA: I kept learnin' words.

MRS CLARK: I was right?

SYLVIA: Yes. But you was wrong too.

GRADY: Hey. Lou. You seen that?

KRAUSE: I seen that.

GRADY: Guy oughta not make a turn with a busted taillight like that.

KRAUSE: Nope. Guy oughta sure not do that.

GRADY: I'll pull him over.

KRAUSE: Be right behind you, Tom.

(GRADY *and* KRAUSE *exit. Sounds of motorcycles pulling off. A red police beacon flashes.*)

SYLVIA: Some years after I left there was a time when I seriously took to learnin' words. To gettin' myself a vocabulary. Get that good job. Become what I always wanted. Nurse. An R N.

(Sound of footsteps and then a car door being thrust open. Footsteps running off. GRADY *and* KRAUSE *shout from offstage.* SYLVIA *crosses to blackboard.)*

GRADY: Hey! Hey! Stop or I'll shoot!

(Sound of gunshot)

KRAUSE: Hey!

*(*SYLVIA *writes the word—RUN—on the blackboard.)*

SYLVIA: First verb I remember. Run. To run.

(Dock bell's whistle is heard from offstage. The whistling is elongated and has a distinct blues quality.)

SYLVIA: To run home. Through the woods out back our home in Louisiana

(Dock bell's whistle repeats.)

SYLVIA: Run home when you papa whistles for you. First noun. Papa. Who was life. Who was home. Who was truth. Who was—bakery! Yeah. Tea cakes and sweet things he'd make in the mornin'. Uh-huh. Run home to papa. Me an' my brothers. Second noun. Brothers. I had twelve of 'em. I can hear 'em all. I can hear one real special.

(Sound of footsteps running swiftly through a woods.)

SYLVIA: Younger brother. Danny. Runnin' home. Through the woods out back. Springfield, Louisiana.

(Dock bell's whistle repeats.)

SYLVIA: Papa whistlin' for him. Danny runnin'. I can hear him. Runnin'.

(Sound of footsteps running through woods now segue to footsteps running on cold, packed, squeaky snow. Breathing sounds added.)

SYLVIA: Runnin'. On cold, squeaky snow. Night of February 2nd, 1958. Place called Milwaukee.

(Sound of a car screeching to a halt. Running sounds continue. Car door opens. Slams shut. Added footsteps. More breathing)

SYLVIA: Run Danny!

(Strobe light. Jarring, neutral musical sound. DANIEL BELL runs onto stage. GRADY cuts him off, chases him. KRAUSE enters chase. All at full speed. GRADY closes in on DANIEL BELL, raises his hand, with gun. The gun goes off at the nape of BELL's neck. BELL falls to the ground, dead. GRADY freezes standing over BELL. KRAUSE freezes some distance away. End strobe.)

SYLVIA: To run.
Yeah. I been learnin' words, Mrs Clark. New ones. But I been goin' over the old ones too. Child words. Truth. Lie. Anger. Justice.

(GRADY and KRAUSE break tableau.)

GRADY: Christ!

KRAUSE: Jesus, Tom.

SYLVIA: Night of February 2nd, 1958. Milwaukee. My brother Daniel Bell shot by a Milwaukee police officer name of Thomas Grady. Other officer name of Louis Krause.

GRADY: There's no pulse. God. Louie. What the hell do I do?

KRAUSE: I don't know, Tom.

(HOCHSTAETTER enters. A man in his fifties. He wears a robe and slippers.)

GRADY: He's just a god-damned little nigger kid anyway!

(KRAUSE *notices* HOCHSTAETTER, *who is now very close to the body of* BELL.)

KRAUSE: Hey!

GRADY: Hey! You get on back!

HOCHSTAETTER: I just wanted to see if he was someone I know.

GRADY: You get on back!

HOCHSTAETTER: You want me to go across the street?

GRADY: Into your house!

HOCHSTAETTER: I just wanted to see if—

GRADY: You get the hell out of here!

(HOCHSTAETTER *retreats, exits.* BELL *exits after light change.* MCCAULEY *has entered.* REPORTERS *charge him. Flash of cameras)*

SYLVIA: Next mornin'.

REPORTER #1: Mister McCauley! You got a statement?

SYLVIA: To run. To run a city. Yeah, that District Attorney Mister McCauley had a statement. For the press.

MCCAULEY: Both officers felt they were pursuing a felon and had a right to shoot under the circumstances. Patrolman Grady was in imminent danger of his life or serious injury due to the knife slashing of that man. At the present time, I see no reason for an inquest.

REPORTER #2: What about their conduct?

MCCAULEY: When the officer's conduct is in good faith and when they were pursuing the reasonable fulfillment of their duties as officers, that is a defense under the Wisconsin statutes.

REPORTER #1: Hasn't the Bell family come forward?

McCAULEY: I've been informed by an attorney for the Bell family that a witness or two have been found. I'll talk with them tomorrow and if their story is any different, I'll order a Coroner's Inquest.

SYLVIA: We met with Mister McCauley the next day.

(McCAULEY *exits amidst hubbub of reporters.*)

SYLVIA: And other witnesses did say different. So some time after, the Medical Examiner held himself a press conference too.

(LaMONTE *has entered and* REPORTERS *now rush to him.*)

REPORTER #1: Mister LaMonte!

LaMONTE: Inquest is scheduled for Friday, 9:30 A M.

REPORTER #2: What's the problem?

LaMONTE: Just some conflicting statements between officers and some witnesses. Also—

REPORTER #1: What about the officers' reports? These distances.

LaMONTE: There is some discrepancy in the officers' statements as to the distance at which the shot was fired. Sheriff Michalski has hand picked a blue ribbon jury—

REPORTER #2: Is it all white?

LaMONTE: Hand picked a blue ribbon jury of prominent Milwaukeeans representing a cross-section of this city. We got a Vice-President of the Northwestern Mutual Life Insurance Company, President of the Wisconsin State Federation of Labor, secretary of one of the city's principal furniture stores, a member of the staff of the Milwaukee School Board and a one-time football star with Marquette and the Chicago Bears.

(LaMonte *exits.* Reporters *follow him offstage. General hubbub. Table and chair for Inquest Scene now brought on.*)

Sylvia: I was at that Inquest. Whole lot younger, God knows. But we was all in that room together. Me, my brother Joseph. Our attorney.

(*Attorney* Hamilton *enters.* LaMonte *and* McCauley *are entering and eventually take their places at the desk of the Inquest.* Sylvia *and* Hamilton *use the old school desk as their desk.*)

Sylvia: Rest of the family was down in Springfield, attendin' services for Dan.

LaMonte: Let the record show that the jury has been sworn in this day, February 14, 1958.

Sylvia: Valentine's Day.

LaMonte: Have you any recommendation at this point, Mister McCauley?

McCauley: In view of my function as District Attorney, I have no control over this Inquest.

(Hamilton *rises.*)

Hamiilton: I just wanted to ask—

LaMonte: Yes, Mister Hamilton.

McCauley: Mister LaMonte. I think the jury should know the nature of these proceedings in more detail as to the function of the District Attorney and Mister Hamilton.

(McCauley *sits.* LaMonte *addresses the jury.*)

LaMonte: Yes. This is a Medical Examiner's fact finding inqui—

(LaMonte *notices that* Hamilton *is still standing. He pauses and stares at* Hamilton *until* Hamilton *sits.*)

LaMonte: A Medical Examiner's fact finding inquiry. The Medical Examiner being myself. This is not a court trial. It is your duty to determine when, where, how and in what manner Daniel Bell came to his death and whether or not that death was due to unlawful means or whether it was justifiable. There will be no cross-exanimation by any attorneys. The only ones that will be authorized to ask questions of the witnesses are the District Attorney and myself. Mister Hamilton, there, represents the Bell family. If they want to, they may suggest a question by writing and submitting it to Mister McCauley or myself. If it is pertinent, the question will be asked.

(Inquest freezes. VORPAGEL, *a detective, has entered and stands U S. Sound of wind is heard. Cold night. He holds a notepad and writes on it.)*

VORPAGEL: Grady. Grady!

*(*GRADY *enters. In uniform)*

GRADY: Yeah?

VORPAGEL: Get over here. I want to go through it one more time.

GRADY: Yeah.

VORPAGEL: All right. You shot from here.

GRADY: Yeah.

VORPAGEL: From this chunk of ice Detective Hughes and I placed here.

GRADY: Yeah.

VORPAGEL: And the kid was over there. Running.

GRADY: Yeah.

VORPAGEL: You warned him.

GRADY: Yeah.

VORPAGEL: You fired.

GRADY: Yeah.

VORPAGEL: He dropped straight down.

GRADY: Yeah.

VORPAGEL: All right. All right, you go back and fill out your report.

GRADY: Yeah. Okay.

VORPAGEL: Yeah. Okay.

(GRADY starts to exit.)

VORPAGEL: Tom?

GRADY: Yeah?

VORPAGEL: You ever fired your gun before?

GRADY: No. Um, I mean, not in the line of duty.

VORPAGEL: All right. Shaffer's ready to take you back.

(GRADY freezes. He is now located about halfway between the spot where he shot BELL during the chase and the spot he just pointed out to VORPAGEL. VORPAGEL enters Inquest as Inquest unfreezes. He sits on the witness chair.)

LAMONTE: You talked with Patrolman Grady. Is that right?

VORPAGEL: I took a chunk of ice and placed it where he told me he had been standing. Detective Hughes and I then measured the distance.

LAMONTE: And what was that?

VORPAGEL: Twenty-three feet, nine inches.

(Freeze Inquest.)

SYLVIA: Wait a minute. Let me get this straight. *(She has gone to spot where GRADY and VORPAGEL were standing together.)* We got the chunk of ice. Here. And…

(SYLVIA crosses to where BELL was shot in original tableau. BELL has appeared again and lies on the floor.)

SYLVIA: We got Dan…here. So Mister Grady'd be standin' over there. According to Detective. Okay? Right? Mister Grady? You want to move back and make it right?

(GRADY *hesitates.*)

SYLVIA: Go on. Twenty-three feet, nine inches.

(GRADY *moves back to that distance.*)

SYLVIA: Thank you. And…point your gun.

(GRADY *upholsters his gun and points it at* BELL.)

SYLVIA: Thank you. Like the reporter asked earlier. What about the police reports? What about the distances? Distances! Not distance.

(SYLVIA *sits and Inquest unfreezes.*)

MCCAULEY: Were Officers Grady or Krause present when these measurements were made?

VORPAGEL: No. They had been taken back to the Safety Building.

MCCAULEY: So Officer Grady was not there when you and Detective Hughes measured the distance.

VORPAGEL: He was not exactly there the first time. But I had put a chunk of ice in the road. Where Grady told me he was standing when he shot.

MCCAULEY: But that was an approximation of distance.

VORPAGEL: It was an approximation.

LAMONTE: Did you see any foreign objects around the body?

VORPAGEL: No.

LAMONTE: Were you present at any time when another investigating officer, Officer Randa, picked up any object?

VORPAGEL: Apparently he had done so immediately prior to my arrival.

LAMONTE: There was no pocket knife near the individual?

VORPAGEL: Right.

LAMONTE: So what'd you do?

VORPAGEL: After the ambulance left, I started asking what had taken place. I instigated a check of various residences. It was disclosed in my report that approximately twelve residences in the area were interviewed and none of them saw or heard anything.

LAMONTE: Thank you. Detective Vorpagel.

(BRADSHAW *enters. He sits.*)

BRADSHAW: I was drivin' along, comin' down Sixth Street.

LAMONTE: Mister Eugene Bradshaw.

BRADSHAW: Come to the corner of Sixth and Wright. When I saw a man run by. Movin' pretty fast. He ran by the front of my car. Then along back. I had pulled up to the arterial there.

(BELL *is standing now in tableau.* KRAUSE *enters and points gun at* BRADSHAW. BRADSHAW *reacts by going to witness chair.*)

KRAUSE: I'm a police officer and I am commandeering this car. Now you make a u-turn and go up this street.

BRADSHAW: This guy do somethin' wrong?

KRAUSE: You see that other officer runnin' up there?

(GRADY *adopts frozen running position in tableau.*)

KRAUSE: When you get by him, you pick him up.

LAMONTE: Then you picked up the other officer?

KRAUSE: Tom. Tom! It's me! Get in!

GRADY: Kid runs like a deer.

KRAUSE: Now listen. You take a right here.

LAMONTE: And you continued going up Sixth Street?

KRAUSE: You take a right turn here.

BRADSHAW: They told me to take a right turn.

LAMONTE: Told you to take a right?

KRAUSE: That's it. Now you take a left here and go up one block.

LAMONTE: So you were going—

BRADSHAW: I was goin' North again, only one block over.

KRAUSE: Now take another left.

BRADSHAW: Then they told me to take another left. Then another. So I was again comin' down Sixth Street. Goin' South just like before.

KRAUSE: Here he comes now.

GRADY: Yeah. I seen that too.

LAMONTE: Did you see anyone?

BRADSHAW: I saw a fellow walkin'. Towards us. North.

LAMONTE: Where was he?

(BELL *is now miming a slow walk.*)

BRADSHAW: East side of the street.

GRADY: Let's go!

KRAUSE: I'm right behind you, Tom.

(KRAUSE *exits.* GRADY *and* BELL *remain in tableau.*)

LAMONTE: Then what?

BRADSHAW: The officers got out in kind of a hurry and when the man saw them he started to run up into the yard to the private walk.

LAMONTE: What happened then?

BRADSHAW: I saw the shot fired and I pulled away.

LAMONTE: Tell us about the shot that was fired.

BRADSHAW: Well. Looked like it was fired in the yard.

LAMONTE: In the yard?

BRADSHAW: He was close enough to catch the man.

MCCAULEY: Catch him?

BRADSHAW: Subdue him in some kind of way without shooting.

MCCAULEY: How?

BRADSHAW: That's his business.

MCCAULEY: That's his business?

BRADSHAW: He should know how to subdue a man.

MCCAULEY: You didn't know the man had a knife in his hand.

BRADSHAW: No, I didn't know that.

LAMONTE: You didn't actually see the officer shoot this man. You heard a shot and saw the officer.

BRADSHAW: I couldn't view the victim as he was shot. The officer was kinda blockin' my view.

LAMONTE: Then you couldn't tell whether this man had a knife or not.

BRADSHAW: I didn't see any knife, no. I saw all this from my car. I didn't get out of my car. He had to be—

LAMONTE: Not "Had to be", what did you see?

BRADSHAW: Saw the shot fired and figured he was close enough to catch the man.

LAMONTE: Catch him if he put his arm out?

BRADSHAW: No, I wouldn't say that.

LAMONTE: Could the officer have jumped on his back?

BRADSHAW: No.

LAMONTE: Catch him with a flying tackle?

BRADSHAW: No.

LAMONTE: Well now if he couldn't make a flying tackle, couldn't jump on his back, couldn't reach him with his arm, the officer would have to find another way to stop him wouldn't he?

BRADSHAW: Well—

LAMONTE: Wouldn't he. Any questions by the jury? Officer Louis Krause.

SYLVIA: Hold it.

(Inquest freezes. SYLVIA goes to tableau where BELL and GRADY are frozen.)

SYLVIA: Got a detective sayin' Grady was over there. And a driver of a police authorized commandeered car sayin' Grady—was there. Good thing they called Officer Krause to clear it all up. After all, Officer Krause wrote in his report that Officer Grady was ten to fifteen feet away. Right Mr. Krause?

(KRAUSE has entered. BRADSHAW exits.)

KRAUSE: Right.

SYLVIA: Then maybe we oughta have Mr.Grady there move in a bit. So he's about ten or fifteen feet away. Don't you think? Mr. Grady?

(GRADY moves in.)

SYLVIA: That's good. Ten or fifteen feet. Thank you.

(SYLVIA returns to her seat at the Inquest.)

LAMONTE: Officer Krause. On the night of February 2nd, how did you run into Officer Grady?

KRAUSE: We passed each other. Just stopped to talk. Have a cigarette.

LAMONTE: Then what happened?

GRADY: Hey, Lou. You seen that?

KRAUSE: Saw the man make a turn with a busted taillight.

GRADY: Guy oughta not make a turn with a busted taillight like that.

KRAUSE: Grady said—he didn't make a hand signal either. We pulled the car over. Grady walked up to the driver and just as he got there the driver's door flew open and Grady jumped back. At this point I noticed the man had something in his hand that glittered.

LAMONTE: Which hand was that?

KRAUSE: The right hand.

(SYLVIA *and* HAMILTON *silently confer.* HAMILTON *writes a question down on a piece of paper.*)

LAMONTE: And the man exited from the car?

KRAUSE: He made a lunge toward Grady and ran maybe fifteen, twenty steps and hollered—I'm a hold up man, you sons-of-bitches will never catch me. He kept running. We took off after him.

(HAMILTON *crosses and gives written question to* MCCAULEY. MCCAULEY *does not read the question. Puts it aside.* HAMILTON *returns to his seat.* LAMONTE's *questioning is continuous through this.*)

LAMONTE: On foot?

KRAUSE: Yes. Grady hollered—stop or I'll shoot. And he fired a round into the air. I got down to the end of the street where he turned and I hollered to stop. I fired a warning shot, then another into the snow bank. The man was now running up Sixth Street and I was getting tired. Grady passed me. I saw this car, got in the passenger's side and explained to the driver that we were chasing a hold up man, and that he should make a u-turn and proceed North.

LaMONTE: And did he?

KRAUSE: The man obliged and we made the u-turn.

LaMONTE: You explained to him?

KRAUSE: Oh, yes sir. That we were chasing a felon. Then I said—as soon as we get up to the other officer we will stop and pick him up. Grady got in. I said—he is on the sidewalk now. Grady says—yeah, I seen that too. And we drove I don't think half a block and we were almost next to him and I told the driver—you stop the automobile right here, we are getting out.

GRADY: Let's go!

LaMONTE: Did either of you have your guns out?

KRAUSE: No. We had holstered them in the car. The car was still in a forward motion when Grady got out and I got out and the driver took off. He was kind of excited, I guess.

GRADY: Stop or I'll shoot!

KRAUSE: Grady jumped on the snow bank and hollered at Daniel Bell to stop. Bell made a lunging swipe at Grady and then I did see what he had in his hand. It was a knife.

LaMONTE: Where was Bell?

KRAUSE: On the sidewalk. *(He gets up and demonstrates.)* See, he made a lunge at Grady and spun back around again and he more or less pivoted on his right foot and started running up the service walk. I hollered stop and just at that moment Grady fired and shot him.

LaMONTE: How close was Grady to Bell at the time of the fatal shot?

KRAUSE: Four. Four or five feet.

SYLVIA: What?

(Inquest freezes.)

SYLVIA: Four or five feet? But your report, which the newspapers even quoted. All right. Mister Grady. Fellow officer sayin'.

(GRADY moves in.)

SYLVIA: 'Bout there. Four, five feet. Thank you.

KRAUSE: Grady put his arm out and he just pulled the trigger and that was it. I would say from the end of the barrel to Bell's back was maybe a foot.

MCCAULEY: Grady shot from about a foot from the victim?

KRAUSE: The end of his hand would be, yes.

MCCAULEY: Now, back when the chase first started. Grady fired a warning shot?

KRAUSE: Yes, sir.

MCCAULEY: How far was that?

KRAUSE: Maybe fifteen or twenty feet.

MCCAULEY: It's possible then to fire right at Bell?

KRAUSE: He didn't fire right at him.

MCCAULEY: He could have.

KRAUSE: He could have dropped him right there if he wanted to.

MCCAULEY: It has been testified earlier today, by Mr. Bradshaw, the driver, that when you picked up Officer Grady you took a right tur—

KRAUSE: I don't know why. Our man was never out of view. We just went straight up Sixth Street.

MCCAULEY: Were there any witnesses to all this?

KRAUSE: The street was deserted. Empty parked cars. Nobody.

McCAULEY: That's all.

LaMONTE: Any questions by the jury? Patrolman—

(HAMILTON *clears his throat as a way of reminding* McCAULEY *and* LaMONTE *of his written questions.* McCAULEY *opens the paper, reads the questions and crumples the paper in his hand.*)

LaMONTE: Patrolman Thomas Grady.

(KRAUSE *exits. Tableau breaks*—BELL *exits.* GRADY *goes to witness chair.*)

LaMONTE: You have the privilege under the Constitution to refuse to answer any and all questions that may tend to incriminate you. Do you wish to waive your rights?

GRADY: I do.

LaMONTE: All right. When you stopped Daniel Bell, did he get out of the car and make a lunge at you with his knife?

SYLVIA: You know Mister Grady.

(GRADY *and Inquest freezes.* SYLVIA *gets up.*)

SYLVIA: When I found out that night, I started dressin' to go down to the Safety Building with my brothers to see what happened—

LaMONTE: Did Daniel Bell make a lunge at you with his knife?

SYLVIA: I see his knife. Oh, he had one. Little one to scrape the bottoms of his feet. And just a few minutes before, when I found out my brother had been shot, when I found out on the television, they showed a picture of Dan's knife on the news -

LaMonte: Did Daniel Bell make a lunge at you with a knife?

Sylvia: And I says to myself—no, it's here. Danny's knife is here. Next mornin', the Milwaukee Sentinel ran a picture of a knife and underneath it said—Daniel Bell's knife. You see, Mister Grady, havin' that knife starin' at me on T V and in the papers—

LaMonte: Did Daniel Bell make a lunge at you with his knife?

Sylvia: Havin' that knife starin' at me!

Grady: I saw the flash of the blade. He had a knife in his right hand. I had to step back quite a bit to avoid being cut. A couple of my friends have been cut quite recently and I wouldn't want something like that to happen to me.

LaMonte: What happened after you entered the car commandeered by Officer Krause?

Grady: We got about parallel to Bell. I jumped out and went over the snow bank and called to the man, the colored man, for him to stop. Bell made a lunge at me again with the knife still in his right hand, attempting to cut me. I stopped, just momentarily enough so that I would avoid being cut. At that point I shot.

LaMonte: Will you describe to this jury just how he lunged at you?

(Grady *gets up to demonstrate, approaches area where tableau had been.* Bell *enters and resumes frozen running position in tableau.*)

Grady: I was running over the snow bank, this way. Mister Bell was on the sidewalk. I called to stop. He went like this... (*He motions with a slashing movement.*) And tried to get over the snow bank to the walk. I drew my gun and shot him. We were very close, maybe inches away from the end of the gun.

(GRADY *now standing in tableau with gun "inches" away from* BELL.)

MCCAULEY: After you fired was his body propelled forward in any way?

GRADY: One more step. Not quite a ways. Then fell forward lengthwise.

(BELL *falls to the floor, slowly.*)

MCCAULEY: What did you do after that?

GRADY: Holstered my gun and ran to the man to see if I could render first aid of any kind if he was hit.

SYLVIA: If he was hit?!

(*Inquest freezes.* SYLVIA *rises and approaches tableau.*)

SYLVIA: Mister Grady. You sayin' the gun was inches away. Gun goes off. Man drops straight down in front of you. And you was wonderin' if he was hit? Any questions by the jury? Hey! Jury! When was you goin' to ask any questions? All sittin' there fumblin' with you blue ribbons.

(VORPAGEL *re-enters tableau.*)

VORPAGEL: Grady!

MCCAULEY: Do you know a detective by the name of Vorpagel?

(GRADY *now back to witness chair.*)

GRADY: I do.

VORPAGEL: I want to go through it one more time.

MCCAULEY: Did you point out to him where you were standing when you shot Mister Bell?

VORPAGEL: You shot from here.

GRADY: I don't believe I did.

MCCAULEY: You heard his testimony.

GRADY: There must have been some confusion because where I showed him, that was where I got out of the car.

VORPAGEL: From this chunk of ice Detective Hughes and I placed here.

GRADY: That was where I got out of the car.

MCCAULEY: I took a statement from you earlier this week.

GRADY: Yes.

MCCAULEY: I asked you how far Bell was from when he knifed at you the last time.

GRADY: I said six feet. But since that time, I have had a chance to go back and check the scene where it was and I realized that he was actually much closer than six feet.

MCCAULEY: You did say six feet at the time.

GRADY: I did, but—

MCCAULEY: Now you say you were practically on top of him or he was close enough to slice you with his arm outstretched.

(HAMILTON *again delivers a written question to* MCCAULEY's *desk.*)

GRADY: That's correct.

MCCAULEY: But he did not hit you?

GRADY: No, sir.

MCCAULEY: Did he come close?

GRADY: Very close. I was afraid for my life.

MCCAULEY: You didn't want to be maimed.

GRADY: No, sir.

MCCAULEY: Did you shoot to kill?

GRADY: No, sir.

(A COURT ATTENDANT *enters with an envelope that carries a knife.)*

MCCAULEY: Do you recognize this knife?

GRADY: That is the knife Mister Bell had in his right hand when he attempted to cut me. Twice.

MCCAULEY: Were you close enough to tackle him?

GRADY: Probably so, but I was scared to with a man with a knife in his hand.

(By this time, GRADY *has worked his way over to the tableau. Although he has his gun out and has extended his arm behind* BELL's *neck, he has not yet brought the gun all the way "down.")*

MCCAULEY: What shirt length do you wear?

GRADY: About a thirty-three.

*(*GRADY's *arm is extended behind* BELL, *but his hand and the gun are perpendicular to his arm.)*

MCCAULEY: But that wouldn't necessarily be your arm.

*(*GRADY *now brings his arm and gun down so the barrel is at the nape of* BELL's *neck.)*

GRADY: My hand would be another seven, eight inches.

*(*HOCHSTAETTER *enters as before, with robe.)*

HOCHSTAETTER: We heard a shot, my son and I.

MCCAULEY: That's all, Officer Grady.

LAMONTE: Mister William Hochstaetter.

HOCHSTAETTER: So I put on my slippers and went out. I saw a man lyin' on the private sidewalk. There was two officers there. I wanted to see if he were black or white. I looked at his hands to see if he were black or white. Maybe a neighbor. That's why I looked at his hands.

(Inquest is frozen again. HOCHSTAETTER *is speaking to* SYLVIA. VORPAGEL *has also appeared again.)*

VORPAGEL: I instigated a check of various residences. It was disclosed in my report that approximately twelve residences in the area were interviewed and none of them saw or heard anything.

SYLVIA: Nobody questioned you that night?

HOCHSTAETTER: No. I saw the story in the paper. Thought I'd better come forward.

*(*SYLVIA *is now checking through some court documents.)*

SYLVIA: You looked at Dan's hands.

HOCHSTAETTER: Yes.

SYLVIA: But at the Inquest they kept asking you questions. Were the hands flat?

HOCHSTAETTER: Flat, I says.

SYLVIA: Palms down?

HOCHSTAETTER: Palms down, I says.

SYLVIA: See any object?

HOCHSTAETTER: None at all. I tell them.

SYLVIA: Would you have seen a knife?

HOCHSTAETTER: Not if it was under his hands. But I looked at his hands. To see if he was black or white. And I didn't see no knife.

SYLVIA: They didn't listen to you.

HOCHSTAETTER: Just kept right on asking me questions.

(Tableau dissolves. SYLVIA *now goes to where* BELL *was and obtains his coat.* HOCHSTAETTER *approaches and sits in the witness chair.)*

LAMONTE: Did he have a coat on?

HOCHSTAETTER: Yes.

LaMonte: How long was the coat?

Hochstaetter: That I don't remember.

Sylvia: Three-quarter length top coat. Light grey.

LaMonte: You looked at his legs?

Hochstaetter: Yes.

LaMonte: What were the color of his shoes?

Hochstaetter: I don't know.

Sylvia: Black. Oxfords. White socks.

McCauley: You said before in your testimony that the sidewalk was clear of snow.

Hochstaetter: That walk was clear, yes.

McCauley: Wasn't it full of snow?

Hochstaetter: No.

(Court Attendant *enters with picture of scene.*)

McCauley: I'd like to show you a picture of what you saw. The walk that's depicted in that picture is full of snow, is it not?

Hochstaetter: That's full of snow.

McCauley: Take a look at the picture again.

Hochstaetter: There is snow there.

McCauley: So you are mistaken about that? He wasn't lying on the clear sidewalk?

Hochstaetter: No.

McCauley: That's all.

Hochstaetter: That was all.

Sylvia: No. Powder blue sport coat, checkered red shirt, striped and brown trousers with a red belt. That was all.

Hochstaetter: I looked at his hands.

(HOCHSTAETTER *exits.* WILSON *enters and takes* BELL'*s coat from* SYLVIA. *He drapes it over the witness chair.*)

WILSON: I made an examination of the outside surface of the coat.

SYLVIA: Charles Wilson. Superintendent of the Wisconsin State Crime Laboratory.

WILSON: Examination in the vicinity of the center seam, midway between the shoulders. There was a smudging of the outside surface in what appeared to be powder residues.

(WILSON *goes to* GRADY *and* BELL *in tableau. He twists the gun into the correct position during the next line. Gun is almost flat on* BELL'*s back, near the nape of* BELL'*s neck.*)

WILSON: The gun would be located about like… that. We obtained six particles of lead. Very small fragments.

MCCAULEY: Could that gun have been fired at the wearer of that coat from fifteen or twenty-three feet away?

WILSON: Impossible.

LAMONTE: The shot fired was touching the fabric of the back of the topcoat?

WILSON: The muzzle was.

LAMONTE: The cylinder was approximately three inches—

WILSON: One inch or less.

SYLVIA: That!

(*Inquest freezes.*)

SYLVIA: That was what they was workin' at. 'Cause the ballistics test didn't come in for days. And by then they'd made all their reports. But that bullet couldn't lie like they could. So they had to shorten, make everything seem shorter than what anybody'd said. Shorter, shorter. And—

(VORPAGEL *enters and there follows a quick recreation of the distances.*)

VORPAGEL: You shot from here.

(GRADY *moves and follows distances according to tableau.*)

GRADY: Yeah.

VORPAGEL: Twenty-three feet, nine inches.

KRAUSE: My first report said he shot from ten or fifteen feet. Later, I realized it was four or five.

GRADY: First, I said it was five or six feet. Then, I realized it was closer.

MCCAULEY: How long's your shirt length?

GRADY: Thirty-three inches. And my hand's another seven, eight inches.

WILSON: One inch or less.

(*Tableau and Inquest dissolve. Stage clears.* SYLVIA *freezes* MCCAULEY *after going to table and picking up her written questions.*)

SYLVIA: Mister McCauley. Mister McCauley! Mister McCauley! Look at these. Look at these!

(MCCAULEY *has dropped the crumpled papers.* SYLVIA *picks them up.*)

SYLVIA: Our questions. You folks said we could ask questions if they was pertinent. An' all along you kept talkin' about that knife bein' in my brother's right hand. 'Bout him slashin' at Grady with his right hand. Right hand! Right hand!

(SYLVIA *has forced the crumpled papers into* MCCAULEY's *hand.*)

SYLVIA: My brother was left hand! Pertinent?

(MCCAULEY *drops the crumpled questions to the floor.*
Exits. SYLVIA *alone. She goes back to her desk and lifts up*
the satchel of books she brought in at the beginning.)

SYLVIA: And that's when I started accumulating all
this stuff. Papers. Books. Court records. Transcripts.
Birth certificates. Death certif… (*Pause*) Yeah. That's
when they changed this. My brother's death certificate.
Where before it said—homicide—they changed it.
Added a word. More words you get, smarter you are.
Right, Mrs Clark? They added—justifiable.

(*Stage darkens. Voices heard from off-stage. Small light on*
crumpled questions.)

BLACK PERSON #1: Justifiable?

BLACK PERSON #2: Is that right?

BLACK PERSON #3: Not justifiable.

BLACK PERSON #4: That's what the paper say.

BLACK PERSON #5: How could it have been?

(BLACK PERSONS *now enter on their lines.*)

BLACK PERSON #4: And the T V, too.

BLACK PERSON #1: Justifiable?

BLACK PERSON #2: I don't believe it.

BLACK PERSON #4: You'd better believe it.

BLACK PERSON #3: Was a whitewash is all.

BLACK PERSON #4: Well, he was a colored man.

BLACK PERSON #1: You got that right.

BLACK PERSON #5: Justifiable.

BLACK PERSON #4: Uh-huh.

BLACK PERSON #5: I'll tell you what'd be justifiable.

BLACK PERSON #1: Tell it.

BLACK PERSON #3: Don't have to.

BLACK PERSON #4: Sure don't.

BLACK PERSON #2: Justifiable.

(BLACK PERSONS *continue talking among themselves.*
BLACK PREACHER *enters. Talks from a podium.*)

BLACK PREACHER: Now folks. Now, now, folks. If I
could just get y'all's attention for a moment.

(BLACK PERSONS *grow silent and turn to* BLACK
PREACHER.)

BLACK PREACHER: Now I know y'all riled up about this
justifiable business. I know y'all upset. But there ain't
no sense in arguin' among yourselves. That's about
like sittin' by an' just complainin'. Like layin' out flat
an' lettin' somebody just walk all over you without so
much as a "pardon me".
An' we all know how much that can hurt. We all know
how much self-respect can be squeezed out in the
process. An' that's why I say it's about time we stop
just sittin' by an' start doin' somethin'!

(BLACK PERSONS *react.*)

BLACK PREACHER: About time we took a stand. About
time we let our voices be heard in the truly public
arena. Not just in the privacy of our churches and clubs
and little bitty living rooms. And so, we are callin' for a
prayer of protest for this Sunday afternoon.

(BLACK PERSONS *react.*)

BLACK PREACHER: Yeah. That's right. I expect from
two to three thousand Negroes to meet at North Sixth
Street and West Vine Streets at two P M and march to
MacArthur Square to pray for justice and the good of
all mankind.

(BLACK PERSONS *react.*)

BLACK PREACHER: Of course…of course, this
pilgrimage is not restricted to Negroes. Anyone who

believes in justice is invited to join. The point is to
be there, to truly be there. Now, we are callin' this
meeting in the widespread criticism and even a threat
against my life.

BLACK PERSON #1: A threat?

BLACK PERSON #2: No!

BLACK PREACHER: Yes, indeed. An anonymous
telephone threat that if I announced the date of the
prayer, I would never walk out of my church alive.

BLACK PERSON #3: But you here.

BLACK PERSON #4: Sure is.

BLACK PERSON #5: And so are we.

BLACK PERSON #4: We behind you.

BLACK PERSON #2: Behind you all the way.

BLACK PREACHER: Thank you, brothers and sisters. I do
thank you truly. 'Cause we Negroes have got to start
speakin' up more for our rights.

(BLACK PERSONS *respond.*)

BLACK PREACHER: Have got to start seein' to it that
freedom is preserved and justice well-served. There
cain't be no more turnin' back. Cain't be no more hidin'
under the covers or just lookin' up all helpless and
defeated. Cain't be no more poor you and poor me and
ain't it a shame why don't we just wait and see.

(BLACK PERSONS *respond.*)

BLACK PREACHER: No. Uh-uh. 'Cause every last one of
us know that if it happens once it can surely happen
again. Like the good Assemblyman done already said:
"There is no difference between shooting Dan Bell in
the back and lynchin' young Emmett Till in Mississippi
in '55."

(BLACK PERSONS *respond.*)

BLACK PREACHER: And there wasn't much difference in the pickin' of the jury either!

(BLACK PERSONS *respond.*)

BLACK PREACHER: So are you with me now?

(BLACK PERSONS *respond.*)

BLACK PREACHER: Can I count on you now?

(BLACK PERSONS *freeze.* CHIEF JOHNSON *appears on a separate area of the stage.*)

JOHNSON: Milwaukee police officers risk their lives hundreds of times a year to safeguard the lives of citizens.

BLACK PREACHER: Now, of course, Chief Johnson is one of the finest persons I ever sat and talked with.

JOHNSON: There can never be a Gestapo or secret police here because we are your policemen.

BLACK PREACHER: He is in the right place.

JOHNSON: We belong to you.

BLACK PREACHER: The right place by appointment.

JOHNSON: I urge Negroes to respect the uniform of the police.

BLACK PREACHER: But he made a bad choice.

JOHNSON: And help the police by teaching your children…

BLACK PREACHER: A truly bad choice.

JOHNSON: To respect the law.

BLACK PREACHER: When he refused to fire Grady!

(BLACK PERSONS *respond.*)

BLACK PREACHER: And that point's gonna be made loud and clear!

(BLACK PERSONS *begin chanting —Protest! Protest!—it*
steadily increases in intensity.)

JOHNSON: Dispel the suspicion, hatred and fear that
must be in some of your hearts.

BLACK PREACHER: 'Cause we are in the right and we're
gonna stand up to the supposed might.

JOHNSON: Just dispel it. Wipe it away.

BLACK PREACHER: We know our mind and we're gonna
be right on time.

JOHNSON: For the man who lives by violence is going to
die that way.

(BLACK PERSONS *now chanting at feverish pitch.* SYLVIA
shouts over them.)

SYLVIA: Reverend! Reverend!

(BLACK PERSONS *and* BLACK PREACHER *grow silent and*
turn to SYLVIA.)

BLACK PREACHER: Yes, sister?

SYLVIA: What happened then?

(MAYOR ZEIDLER *appears.* BLACK PERSONS *turn their*
attention to ZEIDLER.)

ZEIDLER: As your Mayor, I called that conference with
Chief Johnson at the request of several aldermen who
said they had received calls from constituents who
were concerned about the prayer meeting.

SYLVIA: I said what happened, Reverend?

ZEIDLER: There is some fear that although no one
would attempt to break up the rally, trouble would
develop from it.

SYLVIA: What happened?

ZEIDLER: I have confidence that Chief Johnson can
maintain order, though.

(JOHNSON *exits.*)

SYLVIA: Reverend!

ZEIDLER: I am also concerned that the meeting will aggravate rather than diminish the problem of race relations.

SYLVIA: Answer me, please!

BLACK PREACHER: Brothers and sisters, I've…I've called off the protest march.

(BLACK PERSONS *react.*)

BLACK PREACHER: Now wait. I've called it off because it's in the best interest of both Negroes and whites.

(BLACK PERSONS *react.*)

BLACK PREACHER: I just…

ZEIDLER: Still, we do not want to stop peaceable assembly.

BLACK PREACHER: I just fear that some "influences" might creep in and that the meeting might get out of hand.

ZEIDLER: As far as I am concerned…

BLACK PREACHER: Instead, I am calling for a meeting of general prayer.

ZEIDLER: I will work toward reducing group tensions.

BLACK PREACHER: To be held at the church Sunday at two P M.

ZEIDLER: For equal enforcement of the laws.

BLACK PREACHER: Now the church holds about eight-hundred folks.

ZEIDLER: And for the protection of all citizens.

BLACK PREACHER: And I'll be truly disappointed if it's not filled.

SYLVIA: And was it filled?

BLACK PREACHER: We had about a hundred and twenty-five folks.

ZEIDLER: Still, I am of the opinion that the Reverend…

BLACK PREACHER: A fine, fine prayer meeting.

(BLACK PERSONS *begin to leave.*)

ZEIDLER: Could better serve his purpose of improving group feeling by conducting the meeting at his church.

BLACK PREACHER: No, wait. We're still making plans for a march and protest in the future.

SYLVIA: When?

BLACK PREACHER: No date's been set yet.

ZEIDLER: Of course, I'm just expressing my feeling…

BLACK PREACHER: Brothers and sisters, please…

ZEIDLER: That although the situation's not serious…

BLACK PREACHER: Please. Wait.

ZEIDLER: It could be.

BLACK PREACHER: We're still plannin' a march.

ZEIDLER: Without a sense of direction.

(BLACK PERSONS *have all exited.*)

BLACK PREACHER: Justice must be served.

(ZEIDLER *comes toward* BLACK PREACHER *and pats him on the shoulder.*)

ZEIDLER: I just want to give it that sense of direction.

(ZEIDLER *exits.*)

BLACK PREACHER: We did protest, you know. Later on.

(BLACK PREACHER *leaves.* SYLVIA *alone.*)

SYLVIA: So you go home. Think of…home.

(DOCK's *whistle is heard.*)

SYLVIA: First noun. Papa.

(DOCK's *whistle repeats.*)

SYLVIA: Callin' all us kids. Springfield, Louisiana. That whistle you hear? Lord! You hear that an' you better come runnin'. 'Cause that's Papa! He'd say to us—I want you to do such and such a thing an' I want you back in an hour's time. An' when that hour's up, he know it. Without lookin' at a watch. So we might be out back cuttin' pine and he doin' something else. Getting' hay for the cattle, feedin' his hogs, horse, like that. An' we cuttin' pine out back the woods an' stayin' too long. So, there was three whistles he had.

(DOCK's *whistle repeats.*)

SYLVIA: That means we back there too long. You know, horsin' aroun' and all. Then, he go—

(DOCK's *second whistle; a slight variation of the first.*)

SYLVIA: He tellin' us. Y'all better come.

(DOCK's *third whistle: a distinctive blues quality.*)

SYLVIA: He sayin', boy, you all goin' to get it when you come here! An' we sayin'—all right Papa. We comin', we comin'. Man, he blow that whistle so much at us 'til peoples 'round us say he had a whistle for each of his thirteen children. An' we come on home. Uh-huh. Hmm. Come home to that house. Box house he built for hisself in 1911. Carried lumber piece by piece. 'Cause he couldn't, wouldn't get married to Mama 'less he had a place. A home. His own.

(DOCK *enters through doorway. His rocking chair has been placed on the schoolhouse platform that now serves as his porch.*)

SYLVIA: Come out. Sit on that front porch. Take us in his lap, nights. Bugs 'n frogs all singin'.

(*Audio of crickets, frogs.*)

SYLVIA: Papa singin' too.

(DOCK, *seated in the rocker, catches an imaginary and very young* SYLVIA *running by. Lifts her up and places her on his knees. He rocks in his chair.*)

DOCK: Whoa! Now there's my little girl. You have a good day? Papa have a good day. An' Mama. She havin' a busy day, I been told. Bringin' us another child in there, I been told. So, we's all waitin' out here—I been told. That lady friend of you Mama's. Mose Ella. Shew! Take over a man's house like pancake batter spreadin' about a pan. (*He rocks in the chair.*) Gonna be another boy, Sylvia. Got that feelin'. We gonna name him Dan. Daniel. (*He rocks.*) Know how Daniel come here? Come in a song. That's how. Song.

Oh...
The one, two, three
An' the Daddy got the flea
An' the flea bit Mama
And one, two, three.

Oh...
The one, two, three
An' I bounce ya on my knee
An' the knee feels good
An' says—Sylvie!
(*Kisses her, hugs her. Laughs. Rocks*) All them brothers of yours. One, two, three they come. One, two, three in bunches they come. Just like the flea bit Mama.

(*Ready to sing again.* DOCK *hears a stick break in the woods. Footsteps.*)

DOCK: Oh...
The one, two, three
An' your Daddy got the flea...

(*Another stick breaks.*)

DOCK: An' the flea bit Mama
An' one, two, three…
Sylvia… *(Lifting her off his lap. Keeping his eyes straight ahead)* You go inside. Go on. *(He obtains a shot gun from inside the house. Closes door)* Who's out there? This Dock Bell's land. Say your name!

(TUCKER edges onto stage.)

TUCKER: Dock Bell!

DOCK: Yeah?

TUCKER: I come to get my money back.

DOCK: That you, Mr. Tucker?

TUCKER: God-damned right about that, Dock.

DOCK: You been drinkin' a little tonight?

TUCKER: Been drinkin' a lot. You sold me that god-damned cow and calf and that calf ain't worth a shit.

DOCK: Now, Mister Tucker—

TUCKER: You in trouble Dock.

DOCK: That calf's good.

TUCKER: Shit!

DOCK: You been givin' it sweet feed like I tol' ya?

TUCKER: Sweet feed! What the hell difference is—

DOCK: Sweet feed what they like. You mix them oats with molass—

TUCKER: I don't need no dumb ass nigger tellin' me what to feed my stock!

DOCK: Maybe I get some white fella tell ya then.

TUCKER: Shut your mouth, boy!

DOCK: Anyhow, your critters known not to look so good!

TUCKER: I want my money right now!

DOCK: I come by tomorrow. Show you how to mix sweet feed.

TUCKER: My money!

DOCK: That calf's fine.

TUCKER: You cheat me, Dock Bell!

DOCK: Whoa! (*He rises from rocker.*) Dock Bell don't cheat no man.

TUCKER: Only thing worse dealin' with a dumb ass nigger and that's gettin' cheated by a dumb ass nigger!

DOCK: Now you back off, Tucker. Ruth in there havin' a baby. Now you back off.

TUCKER: Baby? Just what we god-damned need. More of them black-assed little niggers runnin' around!

(DOCK *lets off a shot over* TUCKER's *head.* TUCKER *runs off stage.*)

DOCK: They called children, Mister Tucker. Now you go on home. I come by tomorrow and feed that calf proper.

TUCKER: I'm getting' my gun Dock!

DOCK: Yeah? Well I'm gettin' Mose Ella. She takin' care of Ruth. She find out you here and you be breakfast! Mister Tucker? Yoo-hoo? Mister Tucker? No sir. Huh-uh. Dock Bell don't cheat no man. (*He exits.*)

SYLVIA: My Papa didn't cheat no man. Never shot no man. And that Mr. Tucker never did come back that night. Just the thought of Mose Ella comin' at him. My guess. Come back two days later. Asked how to mix sweet feed. We didn't have much trouble with white peoples. A certain understandin'. We not allowed in this place or that. Tell you the truth, those social rules, codes you might want to call 'em, didn't bother us all that much. 'Cept one. That we couldn't have the kind of good school the white people's had. All the State's

fundin' went to white schools. We had to build our
own out of sweat an' love. Lotta sweat, lotta love. But
I tell you, even if you set out to raise yourself by the
bootstraps, you still gotta have a bootstrap to begin
with.

(MRS CLARK *enters.*)

MRS CLARK: It was crowded, girl.

SYLVIA: I know.

MRS CLARK: Had a hundred, hundred-fifty, two
hundred children in this here schoolhouse.

SYLVIA: Grades one through six.

MRS CLARK: All at the same time. Unless a crop needed
pickin'. Then attendance was all haywire. Even then, I
was the only teacher.

SYLVIA: Sayin' more words you get, smarter you are.

MRS CLARK: Ain't that something.

SYLVIA: I never forgot.

MRS CLARK: Oh?

SYLVIA: You was a good teacher.

MRS CLARK: Can't measure that.

SYLVIA: But you was.

MRS CLARK: It was like teachin' in the middle of a
ragin' river. I never knew what they knew. And all the
while tryin' to finish my own schoolin'. Learn what ya
could. That's what is was. Grab on and learn what ya
could.

SYLVIA: I learned a lot.

MRS CLARK: You ain't gonna make me feel better.

SYLVIA: But it weren't your fault.

MRS CLARK: Blind leadin' blind.

SYLVIA: That's not right.

MRS CLARK: Top grade was sixth! Can't go sendin' children out into the world like that.

SYLVIA: Mrs Clark.

MRS CLARK: You was sent out into the world like that! And you was the best of 'em! What! What did you know!?

SYLVIA: Well—

MRS CLARK: Tell me what!

SYLVIA: Knew some nouns. Knew some verbs. I could spell some of 'em an' pick 'em out on paper.

MRS CLARK: What about the rest?

SYLVIA: They all just kinda run together.

MRS CLARK: Black marks all over the page.

SYLVIA: Yeah.

MRS CLARK: And then you an' your brothers go headin' North with all that learnin'.

SYLVIA: Had an Aunt there. Milwaukee. Kept writin' us an' tellin' us. Get yourself up to Milwaukee. Place that's got schools. Place where everybody can get an education. Place where government actually spends money on schools our peoples can go to.

(PATRICK *enters.*)

PATRICK: And they had jobs too.

SYLVIA: Mrs Clark. You remember my brother Patrick.

PATRICK: Then there was this war. Myself. Henry, Eddie, Speedy, that's Lawrence, went over and fought. Europe. Pacific. You meet so many other fellas and hear about other places. You come back home four years later and other places start soundin' pretty good. Places with jobs. 'Cause there weren't none around here. My Papa's land, good as it is, wasn't about to support no thirteen children and they families.

MRS CLARK: So you went up first.

SYLVIA: I did. And my brother Joseph. Patrick came right after. Then we always come home to visit and we might take another brother with us.

PATRICK: We come back to visit one time. Me and my brother Jimmy. About 1950.

(DOCK *enters.)*

DOCK: How you doin' son?

PATRICK: Real good papa.

DOCK: (*offering the rocker)*

Now you sit yourself there.

PATRICK: I can't sit there.

DOCK: You sit there. Big, long drive from Milwaukee. An' you wait what I got. (*He obtains a pan from inside the house.)* Look here.

PATRICK: Tea cakes!

DOCK: Made 'em this mornin' just fo' you and Jimmy.

PATRICK: I tell you they don't have these in Milwaukee.

DOCK: Didn' think they would. (*He pulls up a stool.)* So. How you doin' really?

PATRICK: Getting' by Papa. Getting' by not too bad.

DOCK: Me too. Strawberries comin' up thick all over.

PATRICK: Whoa!

DOCK: An' I tell ya, Danny been a real help. Boy's kinda taken to it.

PATRICK: That's what I come to talk to you about.

DOCK: You mean you gonna come back here? Why we'll raise more strawberries than—

PATRICK: Papa. I got me a decent job in Milwaukee. Real good situation. Otherwise…well I'm a line mechanic. Place called A O Smith. Make frames for cars. Real good job.

(Pause)

DOCK: So. Who else is leavin'?

PATRICK: Danny. Asked me to talk with ya first.

DOCK: Yeah. Yeah. Saw him lookin' at that car of your'n.

PATRICK: It's Jimmy's, Papa.

DOCK: Yeah. That's right. You tol' me that. Didn't take fo' one look when you come in here. We all come runnin' aroun' and sayin' hello. Dan just kinda lookin' at that car there. Saw pictures of hisself drivin' a car like that.

PATRICK: I told him he could stay with me 'til he finds a good job.

DOCK: Oh. Jobs that good up there?

PATRICK: Lot's of 'em. Still need a little luck.

DOCK: Man don't get a job by havin' luck. A trade. You got yourself a trade in the war. Danny ain't got no trade.

PATRICK: He ain't gonna get no trade here, Papa.

(Pause)

DOCK: See to it he gets his rest.

PATRICK: I take care of him. It's just like here only more of things.

(DOCK exiting.)

PATRICK: It's just a city. Ain't got tea cakes is all.

(PATRICK exits. Stage clear except for SYLVIA.)

SYLVIA: So Danny come up North. Fourteen years old and a bigger place he'd never seen. Milwaukee. I tell ya a few things. When peoples ask me what Dan was like, I don't know what to say. I remember him runnin' through the woods back home. I remember him gettin' things for Papa. I remember him sleepin'. Had an ability to nod off any time of day, any place. Like you don't dare be borin' in your talk to him or you soon be talkin' to yourself. Growin' up in Milwaukee, we had to kinda push him. Sometimes a boy don't like to leave bein' young. And then there's that picture he had in his mind. Drivin' a car just like Jimmy's. Come up north and get yourself a job. Wham! Just come up north and get yourself—

(*Knock at the door.* SYLVIA *opens it.*)

SOCIAL WORKER: You must be the sister.

SYLVIA: I'm sorry.

SOCIAL WORKER: I'm from the Milwaukee city welfare department. I have to check a few things.

SYLVIA: Check a few things?

SOCIAL WORKER: You have a brother by the name of Daniel?

SYLVIA: Yes.

SOCIAL WORKER: He was in the office last week to see me and was asking the agency for money.

SYLVIA: Danny applied for welfare money?

SOCIAL WORKER: He was quite demanding about it. It's my job to check these things. People don't always give us the right information. The result can be an unjust thing for working taxpayers…such as yourself.

SYLVIA: What'd Danny say?

SOCIAL WORKER: Well, the last job your brother held was with his brother Patrick. They did junking together?

SYLVIA: 'Til the truck broke.

SOCIAL WORKER: They aren't doing that anymore?

SYLVIA: No money to fix the truck.

SOCIAL WORKER: Before that, Dan worked at the Greenebaum Tannery a few weeks?

SYLVIA: Yes.

SOCIAL WORKER: Then at Wood, Wisconsin for thiry-five dollars a week when he quit to get a better job?

SYLVIA: That's right.

SOCIAL WORKER: Before that, he was in Cleveland a little while.

SYLVIA: Workin' in a restaurant.

SOCIAL WORKER: New York?

SYLVIA: Workin' in a restaurant.

SOCIAL WORKER: Does he have trouble adjusting to these jobs?

SYLVIA: He has trouble makin' a livin' at 'em.

SOCIAL WORKER: When I questioned him about his need for money he said he had to pay his relatives rent.

SYLVIA: Everybody earns their keep around here.

SOCIAL WORKER: I asked him how many people eat in the home and he told us that each one cooks for himself. So he needed the money. Obviously, this doesn't seem to be true since you're here and, no doubt, cook for all the brothers.

SYLVIA: Mmm-hmmm.

SOCIAL WORKER: I'm afraid he can only get aid on a voucher basis because he is still considered a transient.

I can give him sixty-three cents a day for seven days
until we talk with him again. That's a total of four
dollars and forty-one cents to Berlin's Food Market at
935 West Walnut Street. Good day.

(SOCIAL WORKER *hands* SYLVIA *the voucher and exits.*)

SYLVIA: Thing is, you could almost live on that those
days. Almost. But we didn't want Danny getting' that
kind of money. Relyin' on it. So Patrick kinda got on
him. Sat him down. Told him what Papa told him once.

(DOCK *has entered.*)

DOCK: Patrick. Now you sit there. Listen. My first
job was beatin' brick, see. Get a load of bricks, you
understan', and beat 'em with a hammer. Whap, whap,
whap, whap, whap. All day long. You understan'?
Whap, whap, whap, whap, whap. Beat 'em into a
kinda dust. Then I go in to town, see. New Orleans.
And sell it six bits a gallon. Brick dust. Peoples spread
it all over they wooden floors and walk on it, see, you
understan', and kinda grinds it into they floors when
they walk. But when you sweep it off, cleans and
shines they floors real good.

SYLVIA: But Danny was dreamin' somethin' Papa
didn't.

DOCK: Just shined they floors like new!

SYLVIA: Papa's dream was land, wife, home, children.

DOCK: That was work.

SYLVIA: Danny? Picture of hisself comin' up to
Milwaukee, getting' a job right off and drivin' a big ol'
car.

(*Audio: sound of original breathing and running.*)

SYLVIA: But things was just startin' to change. Danny
took a job at the car wash. Rainbow auto wash.

(*Sounds grow louder.* DOCK *about to exit.*)

SYLVIA: But what was special.

DOCK: Just shined they floors like new.

SYLVIA: What was different this time was that at that car wash he was tryin' to organize a union. Probably still wanted that big ol' car, but he was goin' to do somethin' while workin' at getting' it. Takin' somethin' into his own hands,

DOCK: Man, that's work.

SYLVIA: Growin' up. Dressin' different. Proud like.

(Strobe: Replay of original chase with BELL, KRAUSE *and* GRADY. *Shot.* KRAUSE *and* GRADY *exit.* BELL *lies on the floor.* SYLVIA *goes to him. Pause. After, she again starts to speak.* BELL *exits.)*

SYLVIA: I started applyin' one of the words I knew. Anger. We wanted, I wanted, to hurt the city like they'd hurt us. So we sued 'em. At the time, most we could sue for was eighteen thousand dollars. Damages. Loss of Society and Companionship. Them's the legal words. But then another word come to mind. Justice. Justice.

*(*DOCK *calls from off-stage.)*

DOCK: Sylvia?

SYLVIA: Papa had to come up here to testify.

DOCK: I still can't tie these things.

SYLVIA: Lawsuit could only be filed under his name. 'Cause Dan was his son.

*(*DOCK *enters. Loose tie)*

DOCK: Fix this fo' me?

SYLVIA: Here.

*(*SYLVIA *ties* DOCK's *tie for him.)*

DOCK: We doin' the right thing. This suin' business. I know that now.

SYLVIA: Yes, Papa.

DOCK: Lookin' forward to northern justice. Like you been sayin'. Ain't like that down South. Like what Reverend Mr. King goin' through. Judges and juries spittin' 'n' cursin' right in front of 'em. Throwin' 'em in jails. Blowin' peoples up. Settin' fire to they churches. Ain't like that here. They listen to a boy's father.

SYLVIA: Look, Papa. They somethin' you gotta know.

DOCK: What?

SYLVIA: 'Bout these people in Milwaukee. Ones you goin' to talk to today. They educated. They got ways. They—

DOCK: They listen to a Father when he tell 'em about his son.

(DOCK *sits in the chair, center.* SYLVIA *backs off a few steps.*)

SYLVIA: They put him on that stand.

DOCK: They ask me 'bout Dan.

SYLVIA: Ain't no record of that trial. Just my memory.

DOCK: Ask me if Dan was my son. I say—yes. They say—you sure? I say—yes, Danny's my son.

SYLVIA: 'Cause if he weren't his son, we couldn't sue.

DOCK: Why, I was sittin' out on that porch night Danny was born. Mose Ella Richardson took care of Ruth that night. Took Danny in to her hands.

SYLVIA: Milwaukee police investigated real good this time. Sent a detective all the way down to Louisiana. Gonna prepare for this trial. Couldn't find no record of Danny's birth.

DOCK: I don't know records. I mean, Danny's my son.

SYLVIA: How do ya prove somethin' like that?

DOCK: No! Didn't take him from nobody else! If she was alive, Ruth'd tell ya!

SYLVIA: Mama died in '49.

DOCK: Ask my other boys. They all tell ya. Ask Jimmy and Ernest. They three all kinda born together. Played together.

SYLVIA: Kept tryin' to tell 'em.

DOCK: What? What you folks drivin' at?

SYLVIA: On that stand.

DOCK: Now Danny was a quiet child from the night he was born.

SYLVIA: No gun.

DOCK: That's up here in my memory.

SYLVIA: Expectin' Northern justice.

DOCK: Now if that's in my memory, that's the only way I could know that.

SYLVIA: Kept pressin' him.

DOCK: I don't know why there no birth certificate.

SYLVIA: But these peoples wouldn't back off!

DOCK: Gotta be records in Springfield somewhere. You say you was down there checkin'? Maybe ya didn't look in the right place. 'Cause he come from Ruth. And me. Dock Bell. *(He stands.)* An' Dock Bell don't cheat no man. You come to my home. We go right now. I show you where Danny grow up. Where he used to run an' play. Run through the woods out back. An' work hard. I made him work hard. Cuttin' pine. I show you where he had schoolin'. Where he fished. Where he went to get groceries when I send him. For bags of flour. Pails of molasses so's, so's I could mix sweet feed for my stock. I tell ya! He's my boy! He's my boy! *(He collapses into chair.)*

SYLVIA: Papa! *(She gets a blanket and puts it over* DOCK's *lap and legs.)* We took him to the hospital in Milwaukee. County General. Same place as Dan. Then brought him back to Louisiana. The city offered us $1800 settlement. I don't even know why. Trial was all stopped. An' we refused to sign that city check. We got Papa back to his farm. An' Henry was there. Oldest an' first child. Who had stayed in Louisiana all the time. Took care of Papa 'til…

DOCK: Henry?

SYLVIA: 'Til he spoke real different one night.

DOCK: I want you to tell all the children. Dan's grave don't just have earth on it. Got layers an' layers of lies on it.

SYLVIA: Henry told us all.

DOCK: Dan's gonna push those lies. Push clear through. 'Cause what was done in the dark…

(Lights fading on DOCK.*)*

SYLVIA: Papa?

DOCK: Shall one day come to light.

*(*DOCK *dies. Lights out on* DOCK. SYLVIA *alone.)*

SYLVIA: Papa? Papa!

(Lights fade to black.)

END OF ACT ONE

ACT TWO

(Light comes up on SYLVIA *sitting at her desk. Dictionary and paper in front of her. After a moment she looks up.)*

SYLVIA: Mrs Clark?

(Light up on MRS CLARK.*)*

MRS CLARK: Yes, Sylvia.

SYLVIA: Lie.

MRS CLARK: Uh-huh.

SYLVIA: Been lookin' at it from all angles.

MRS CLARK: Tricky word sometimes.

SYLVIA: Don't I know it.

MRS CLARK: English language comin' at you.

SYLVIA: Yes, Ma'am. I mean now just look at this here word "lay", for instance. Sometimes folks might say— Y'all lay on down here and rest a spell.

MRS CLARK: Uh-huh.

SYLVIA: Well, it's funny. 'Cause it says here in the dictionary that you can lay pavement, pipe, plaster, paint, all like that. And you can lay tax on land, lay siege to a town, lay blows to somebody's head. Why, you can even lay the blame for you own wrongdoin' on somebody else.

MRS CLARK: Yes.

SYLVIA: But when you yourself "recline," what you actually doin' is lyin'.

MRS CLARK: Yes.

SYLVIA: Lyin' down, that is. It's lie, not lay.

MRS CLARK: That's right, Sylvia.

SYLVIA: To lie down. To lie in wait. To lie in the grave. To...to make an untrue statement with the intent to deceive. To lie.

MRS CLARK: More words you get...

SYLVIA: Black marks all over the page.

MRS CLARK: Just have to keep at it.

SYLVIA: Yes, but...but when they all gonna come clear? All these black marks, these words. When they all gonna make complete sense? And it ain't like I haven't been tryin', you know. Like I haven't always been tryin'. I...

(DOUGLAS *calls from offstage.* MRS CLARK *exits.*)

DOUGLAS: Mama.

SYLVIA: Was even in California once. Tryin'.

DOUGLAS: Mama, I'm gone.

SYLVIA: Los Angeles.

(SYLVIA *studies.* DOUGLAS *enters.*)

DOUGLAS: Mama.

SYLVIA: Yes, son.

DOUGLAS: I'm gone.

SYLVIA: Me, too. Soon. To the hospital.

DOUGLAS: Afternoon shift today?

(DOUGLAS *has "entered" the room* SYLVIA *is in, but is also about to leave.*)

SYLVIA: Yeah. Sure be glad when I finish my nursin' trainin'.

DOUGLAS: I know, Mama. You'll make it.

(DOUGLAS *kisses* SYLVIA.)

SYLVIA: Where your books?

DOUGLAS: Books?

SYLVIA: Yeah. Ain't you goin' to school?

DOUGLAS: Uh...no. No classes today.

SYLVIA: Don't you usually have classes on Thursdays?

DOUGLAS: Yes, but...

SYLVIA: Then where your books?

(Pause)

DOUGLAS: I don't know, Mama.

SYLVIA: You don't know where your books are?

DOUGLAS: I don't know about all that stuff.

SYLVIA: All what stuff?

DOUGLAS: School...college.

SYLVIA: You've gotta give it some time, son.

DOUGLAS: I've given it time.

SYLVIA: And?

DOUGLAS: It ain't for me.

SYLVIA: And what is?

DOUGLAS: A good job. Some money in my pocket.

SYLVIA: And what you think you in college for?

DOUGLAS: I don't know.

SYLVIA: Now that's the dumbest answer I ever heard.

DOUGLAS: Mama, I...

SYLVIA: What you sayin' to me?

(Pause)

DOUGLAS: I quit school.

SYLVIA: What?

DOUGLAS: Quit school.

SYLVIA: When?

DOUGLAS: Yesterday.

SYLVIA: To do what, may I ask?

DOUGLAS: I joined the Air Force.

SYLVIA: You what?

DOUGLAS: Mama, I wanna go places, see things. I'm not into sitting in no classrooms. I'm not into studying anymore. I want a job, money.

SYLVIA: So you up and join the Army.

DOUGLAS: The Air Force.

SYLVIA: Same difference. Same government. Same war.

DOUGLAS: I probably won't even go to Nam. That's more the Army's thing. The Marines.

SYLVIA: Don't matter 'cause you in it now. In the whole mess.

DOUGLAS: It's just a job, Mama, a career. Just a way to make a living.

SYLVIA: No, it ain't just all that.

DOUGLAS: Well, without college I was bound to be drafted.

SYLVIA: Then stay in college.

DOUGLAS: I hate college.

SYLVIA: Then be like Cassius Clay. Refuse to serve. Or go to Canada. I'd stand behind you. I'd stand behind you all...

DOUGLAS: Now that makes a hell of a lotta sense.

SYLVIA: No!

DOUGLAS: Mama, I...

SYLVIA: Ain't you learned nothin'? Ain't you remembered what they did to your Uncle Dan? How they shot him dead? Shot him dead in his own country and then covered it up? And it's still covered up.

DOUGLAS: What's that got to do with...

SYLVIA: And what about your Uncles Henry, Eddie, Patrick, Speedy? Veterans, they were. Veterans of World War II. Humph. They come back home and couldn't even urinate in a public toilet. And that's this country. This country's doin's.

DOUGLAS: Mama, that was the forties, the fifties. But it's the seventies now. Times have changed. The military's integrated now. Haven't you heard? Been integrated for a long time. There's all kinds of opportunities for advancement, for training, for learning a skill.

SYLVIA: And who told you that? Some white recruiter?

DOUGLAS: He wasn't... *(Pause)* Look. Where will I be if I go to jail? I mean, do I look like the heavyweight champion of the world? And how long would I last in Canada? I like it here. This is my country.

SYLVIA: Then stay in college.

DOUGLAS: No!

(Pause)

SYLVIA: Do you know why I left Springfield, Louisiana?

DOUGLAS: Yes, Mama, you've...

SYLVIA: Do you know why I went up north to Milwaukee?

DOUGLAS: Yes, to get an education. Nineteen years old and nothing but a sixth grade education.

SYLVIA: And I hardly got that. Us walkin' those roads to school. White kids ridin' by in they buses, yellin', screamin', throwin' rocks sometimes, ole bus driver tryin' to run us off the road.

DOUGLAS: Yes, Mama, I know.

SYLVIA: And so I come north and went to work washin' dishes...

DOUGLAS: From two to four and six to eleven each day.

SYLVIA: And took vocational trainin' 'cause I wanted to make somethin' of myself.

DOUGLAS: Mama, I've heard this all before.

SYLVIA: Well, now you just gonna hear it one more time, sit!

(DOUGLAS *sits.*)

SYLVIA: I studied hard, took tests, applied for jobs. Even applied at the police department one time. Can you believe that? But nothin'. Couldn't get nothin' that was worth anythin'. One time they throwed my application in the trash can the minute my back was turned. Another time they said: "Yeah, we know you passed the test with one of the highest marks, but you ain't a high school graduate." "But I'm studyin'," I said. "I'm goin' to school." "But we need graduates." "Please, mister, please, I want, I need this job." Me beggin' those crackers like a fool. And I sees them Polish gals, just come over to this country. Half of 'em could hardly speak English. But they got hired. Yeah, they got hired. 'Cause after all, this is America. This is the damn meltin' pot. The land of opportunity! (*Pause. She goes to* DOUGLAS.) Education, son. It's about education. I want you to get what I didn't get. What this country wouldn't allow me to get.

(*Pause*)

DOUGLAS: I'm sorry, Mama.

SYLVIA: Go on, son. Go on. I ain't got nothin' more to say. 'Sides, you in it now. So you on your own. You out there.

(DOUGLAS *exits slowly.*)

SYLVIA: Douglas.

(DOUGLAS *stops at the door.*)

SYLVIA: Just be careful, son. Be careful.

(DOUGLAS *leaves. Gunshot.* SYLVIA *rushes to the door.*)

SYLVIA: *(Screaming)* Douglas!

(SYLVIA *freezes at the door. Telephone rings.* GRADY *and* KRAUSE *enter, both in civilian clothes and twenty years older than in* ACT ONE. *On opposite sides of the stage.* GRADY *holds a telephone receiver to his ear.* KRAUSE's *telephone rings and he picks it up.*)

KRAUSE: Hello.

GRADY: Hello, Lou?

KRAUSE: Yeah.

GRADY: This is Tom. I just got here to Chicago. They just give me your message.

KRAUSE: Jesus Christ, where the hell have you been?

GRADY: Well, I was out in the world.

KRAUSE: Is that right?

GRADY: Well, we've been a long time getting here. It's been a party.

KRAUSE: You were at a party?

GRADY: No, it's been a party out in the snow.

KRAUSE: I understand that.

GRADY: Where you at here?

KRAUSE: I'm in Milwaukee.

GRADY: Oh, this is Milwaukee?

KRAUSE: Yeah.

GRADY: Oh. I couldn't think of 414. Yeah, that's Milwaukee. What's up?

KRAUSE: Well, let me tell you something, Tom. I got a problem. Can you talk where you're at?

GRADY: Uh, yeah. To a certain extent.

KRAUSE: Well, can you go someplace where I can call you?

GRADY: Uh...this is the only phone here.

KRAUSE: Oh. Well, let me tell you. When I got out of the joint I went to this counselor school.

GRADY: Yeah.

KRAUSE: For, you know, alcoholism.

GRADY: Umhum.

KRAUSE: And drugs. And we had a marathon with two psychologists.

GRADY: Uh-huh.

KRAUSE: And this thing resurfaced with Bell. And I'll be very honest with you, Tom. I haven't slept too much. I've gone to the priest, and you know I didn't mention names or anything else.

GRADY: Uh-huh.

KRAUSE: He mentioned going to an attorney. So I went to an attorney and again kept this very, very quiet.

GRADY: Uh-huh.

KRAUSE: And the only thing he tells me is to go to the district attorney.

(GRADY *is speechless for a moment.*)

GRADY: About what?

KRAUSE: Well, about this shooting you and I were involved in.

GRADY: Yeah.

KRAUSE: This thing resurfaced and man I'll tell ya. If we would have told the truth from the beginning, everything would be gone. Be over and done with.

GRADY: Yeah. Yeah, I can't talk on that here.

KRAUSE: I really don't know what to do and I thought I would call you and see what you can...what your advice is.

GRADY: Well, the way I see it, everything is over and done with and, and that's it. And you know anything up now, well, the repercussions and the problems for everybody way down the line and...oh, man. It would be inconceivable what could happen.

KRAUSE: Well, that's what I'm thinking of too. But then as I told a few other people that night, let's tell the goddam truth and let's get it over with and done with.

GRADY: But you know how things go. Do you remember, uh, everybody down there. I can't mention all the names now, but everybody that backed us, all the way down the line is...oh, man, Christ, there'd be hundreds of people that'd be in the soup.

KRAUSE: I know that. I understand that, Tom.

GRADY: And it's over with and done with now and so it's best just to leave that sleeping dog lay before...

SYLVIA: It's lie. (*She has closed the door and crosses to her desk.*)

GRADY: Man, there'd be a world of hurt coming up. All the way down the line.

KRAUSE: And you know who's going to be hurt the worst. You and I.

GRADY: Yeah. You bet. And we've had it then. We'd be in a sinking boat by ourselves. And boy, it would be sunk. There's no doubt about that one way or at all.

(Lights change as KRAUSE *and* GRADY *hang up their telephones.* GRADY *freezes and lights come up behind* KRAUSE *to revel two* WIRETAPPERS *manning wiretap equipment.* KRAUSE *confers with them.)*

SYLVIA: Louis Krause and Thomas Grady having theyselves a little chit-chat on the telephone. Part of a legal wiretap. Three legal wiretaps made. December first, second, and sixth of 1978. Twenty years later, Mrs. Clark. Twenty years of copin', gettin' by. Douglas in the Air Force, still. Me livin' and workin' in Milwaukee again. All my family doin' this and that, doin' the best they can. And then this. Like somethin' out of a dream. Up through layers and layers of lies. Just like...

(Telephone rings.)

SYLVIA: How did papa know?

*(*SYLVIA *sits with transcript of wiretaps. She reads as* KRAUSE *and* GRADY *speak.* KRAUSE's *phone rings two more times.* WIRETAPPER *signals that equipment is ready.* KRAUSE *answers phone.)*

KRAUSE: Hello.

TELEPHONE OPERATOR: *(On audio)* We have a collect call for anyone from Tom.

KRAUSE: Sure. Where's he calling from?

GRADY: Atlantic, Iowa.

KRAUSE: Atlantic, Iowa? Where in the hell is that, Tom?

GRADY: About half way between Des Moines and Omaha.

KRAUSE: Oh, yeah.

GRADY: Yeah, it's slicker than a goose and the windows are freezing so bad you got that little peephole to go through.

KRAUSE: Yeah.

GRADY: We got a bearcat.

KRAUSE: You just caught me. I was just walking in the door.

GRADY: Yeah. We just pulled in here. It was just twelve o'clock noon so I thought, well, better give you a jingle.

KRAUSE: Yeah, very good.

GRADY: Yeah, you know, Lou, this deal, the darn thing was such a regrettable deal, you know. It was an accident and everything. Nobody would ever believe it was an accident anymore and...you know, when things happen like that in the past, no matter what you do or how you punish yourself for it you just can't set the clock back and do it over. The thing was, is there.

KRAUSE: Uh-huh.

GRADY: And God knows how much both of us have suffered over the damn thing. We lost our jobs, you might say. They hounded us until they got them.

KRAUSE: You see, that's the way I feel. You've been walking around with that cloud over your head and so have I.

GRADY: Yeah, and say like right now I got, well, I'm still screwed up from being laid off. I still owe about a thousand bucks yet. But I'm coming out of it, you know.

KRAUSE: Uh-huh.

GRADY: I got my house built. I got a wife. You know, we'll be married six years this February and we've yet to have the first cross word.

KRAUSE: Uh-huh.

GRADY: That's unbelievable, isn't it?

KRAUSE: Right.

GRADY: And I've got it so good, if something like this would come up now, man, I lose my job. I lose my home. I lose my wife. I lose everything. And you know, that goddam Milwaukee is such a fucked up place. Boy, if you had yourself a car come to Colorado and find something. Jesus Christ, you seemed so happy out there.

(A WIRETAPPER hands KRAUSE a note. KRAUSE reads it.)

KRAUSE: *(To GRADY)* I did.

GRADY: And you know all this is in the past, and digging up this damn dog again, that hits us right square in the eyes. Honest to God, Louie. Now sure...

KRAUSE: The only thing that really bothers me, Tom, is why did you take the knife out of your pocket and put it in the kid's hand? Now this is what really bothers me.

GRADY: Well...

KRAUSE: Now I don't know if that's the reason you carried that knife and if you ever had a mishap like that you'd be protecting yourself or what.

GRADY: I've carried a jackknife since I'm four years old. I got one in my pocket right now.

KRAUSE: Uh-huh.

GRADY: Remember in police training school how they used to always say if something like that comes up, that's the thing to do. So that's what we all thought of that night and we done it.

KRAUSE: See, but that's what really bothers me. I get flashbacks of this goddam thing since this popped out in that marathon and it's goddam near drove me to drink.

GRADY: Yeah.

KRAUSE: And I haven't had a drink in, uh, over three years, Tom.

GRADY: You know, as far as me carrying...remember when the kid was in grade school and you had hightops with the pocket on the side?

KRAUSE: Yeah.

GRADY: Well, man, I was raised in that Third Ward, you know, with all the Guineas. Well, if you didn't have a jackknife in your pocket why nobody talked to you. You know, in our boots.

KRAUSE: Right.

GRADY: And I've always carried one. I never carried it like, you know, say special for an occasion like that or to slit somebody's throat. There was nothing like that, Louie. Nothing foreseen.

KRAUSE: Well, I don't think that even if it did come out that it was pre-meditated, I don't think that you were hunting somebody down like a person would go out and hunt rabbits or pheasants, you know, with the intent.

GRADY: But when...

KRAUSE: You know, the kid ran and didn't say anything. He ran real fast.

GRADY: Yeah, but what's the point of bringing all this up?

(SYLVIA *bolts up from her chair and throws the transcript on the floor. Scene freezes. She stares at* GRADY. *Lights change,* SYLVIA *resumes reading, scene comes to life again.)*

GRADY: See, truthfully what happened was I was going to hit the guy over the head with that thing, see, and it went off. Remember?

(WIRETAPPER *gestures for* KRAUSE *not to remember.*)

KRAUSE: Well, no, I don't remember.

GRADY: Yeah.

KRAUSE: I wasn't, I was still getting out of the car and coming towards you when I heard the gunshot and down he went.

GRADY: See, I was trying to grab him and I had the goddam gun in my hand, and when I grabbed at him the gun banged on him and then I suppose my finger must have been on the trigger and off it went, see. And...you're not recording...

(WIRETAPPER *rips off his headphones and runs up to* KRAUSE. *Eventually,* KRAUSE *signals that everything is okay and* WIRETAPPER *returns to tape recorder.*)

KRAUSE: I would like to discuss this farther with you, Tom. Maybe when you get home or something or you want to...

GRADY: Well, see, I just as soon... Ann don't know nothing about this.

KRAUSE: Right.

GRADY: And we both got a chance now. Why destroy it by bringing out this dead dog? It's just not worth it. It's not worth it. You know, like it's the old story of the little girl who went out and got herself screwed and got knocked up. Well, the old saying, you can get yourself screwed but you can't unscrew them. You know.

KRAUSE: Yeah.

(WIRETAPPER *brings* KRAUSE *another note.*)

GRADY: And that's about what this deal is. We're screwed and we can't get unscrewed, and it's up to... well, we got to live with it whether we like it or not.

KRAUSE: Yeah, but Tom, do you really feel that was an accident?

GRADY: I guarantee you, Lou. Strike me dead, uh, a hundred percent guarantee. Honest to God, Louie. There is no doubt. There's a hundred percent truth in that.

KRAUSE: See, Tom, what really bothers me...

GRADY: See, it's...

KRAUSE: Is I didn't see you bring your hand and your arm down.

GRADY: But that's, so help me, Lou, that was a hundred percent deal. Please, Louie, I beg you. I, if any, God, Louie, don't do it.

KRAUSE: Okay.

GRADY: I'm just pleading with you, Louie, honest to God.

KRAUSE: All right.

GRADY: I tell you, Louis, this would kill my ma. And I wouldn't go through it again. I would take the gas pipe. Honest to God.

KRAUSE: Uh-huh.

GRADY: I'll take the gas pipe before I go through this deal again.

(Scene freezes for a moment. Lights fade out on KRAUSE's *apartment. As* SYLVIA *begins speaking,* GRADY *puts away his phone and stands as if in a courtroom with his right hand raised and left hand on the bible.)*

SYLVIA: After almost a year of investigation by the Milwaukee D A's office—a whole other different

office than the one way back when—Thomas Grady
was charged with perjury and homicide by reckless
conduct. He—pleaded guilty.

GRADY: *(Simultaneously)* Guilty.

SYLVIA: To both charges and was sentence to seven...

GRADY: *(Simultaneously)* Seven years.

SYLVIA: *(Turning and staring at GRADY)* But was out in...

GRADY: Three and a half.

SYLVIA: Three and a half years. Perjury and reckless
conduct. Reckless conduct. *(Looking through some
papers)* Where's that...? *(Finding what she's looking for)*
Here. Number 940.06. Homicide by Reckless Conduct.
Two. Reckless conduct consists of an act which creates
a situation of unreasonable risk and high probability
of death or great bodily harm to another and which
demonstrates a conscious disregard for the safety of
another and a willingness to take known changes or
perpetrating an injury. *(She drops the paper.)* Reckless
conduct? ...He killed my brother, dammit! Shot him in
the back! And they...

GRADY: *(Shouting at SYLVIA)* It was an accident! I swear!

*(SYLVIA says nothing. She sits down in her chair and turns
away from GRADY. He collects himself and pleads his case to
the audience.)*

GRADY: You try to change, to better yourself. You try
to.... And we all make mistakes down the line. Things
happen to us down the line. Every last one of us. And
me? boy, I was hurting back then. Really hurting. I
mean, the job was important to me. My oldest daughter
had a severe case of polio, and, being unskilled, I
needed a job badly to pay for the many operations
and medical bills. And my first wife, she had filed for
divorce in December of '57, and well, I had just moved
out that next January. She had a temporary alimony

motion laid on me. Half my paycheck for support. Four
young kids—six, five, four, and two years old. And my
second payment was due February 2nd of that year.

(GRADY *and* SYLVIA *now look at each other.*)

GRADY: February 2nd, 1958! (*He now pleads his case to*
SYLVIA.) Look, before all this blew up in my face I was
an over-the-road truck driver for Navaho, see. And my
normal West Coast trip would take me four and a half
days. So it was a sleeper operation. I'd travel with a
partner. One person would drive approximately a five-
hour shift and then go in the bunk right behind and
sleep and the other one would drive five hours. And
Navaho would assign drivers. And of course I drove
with some black drivers.

(SYLVIA *turns away from* GRADY.)

GRADY: Shared the bunk in a sense. "Lived" together,
as it were. Never any troubles. They're good drivers...
black drivers...BLACK!

(SYLVIA *turns to* GRADY.)

SYLVIA: Black. Afro-American. Negro. Colored person.
Darkie. Nig...

(KRAUSE *has entered and overlaps* SYLVIA.)

KRAUSE: Nigger? (*He joins* SYLVIA *and* GRADY.) Look.
Personally, I had fairly good rapport with blacks. I
mean, after the shooting it was Grady who referred to
Bell as just another nigger kid. Not me.

(KRAUSE *and* GRADY *stare at each other.* GRADY *leaves.*
KRAUSE *talks to* SYLVIA.)

KRAUSE: And that phrase has haunted me because I
heard it from police officers when I was on the force
and—more important—from current police officers.
I mean like policemen would approach me then, see.
"He was just a nigger kid," they'd say. And even

today I've been threatened. There've been phone calls and phone calls. I don't know how they get my unpublished number. "It was just another nigger kid," the voice would say. A lot of cops hate me now. They say, "Krause, you're a damned fool. Why did you come forward and tell the truth? It was just a nigger kid."

(LAWYERS *enter, trial desks and chairs are brought out.*)

DEFENSE LAWYER #1: But you had to come forward, isn't that correct?

KRAUSE: Yes.

(KRAUSE *now sits in witness chair.*)

DEFENSE LAWYER #1: Even though you supposedly engaged in silent complicity for twenty years.

KRAUSE: I don't know about all that.

DEFENSE LAWYER #1: Well, you've stated that.

KRAUSE: Look. Let me explain something about me and February 2nd, 1958, okay? You know, I don't think I even kept a daybook after February 2nd, because I really didn't give a shit, okay? After I walked out of that Detective Bureau and got on that motorcycle, I wanted to pull that motorcycle right out in the middle of the State Street and take off my uniform and walk up State Street and get on a bus and go home in my shorts.

DEFENSE LAWYER #1: Is that so?

KRAUSE: Yes. I wanted to walk up to Chief Johnson's office and resign from the Milwaukee Police Department. That was my intention. Or like I say, pull the motorcycle out in the middle of State Street and take off my uniform and...and urinate all over that motorcycle because I didn't feel justice was being done.

DEFENSE LAWYER #1: But you didn't do that. You stayed on the Police Department. Isn't that correct?

KRAUSE: Yeah, I stayed.

DEFENSE LAWYER #1: Until you were "let go" just two months later for drunken brawling.

KRAUSE: Well, I wouldn't exactly...

(DEFENSE LAWYER #1 *moves to get* KRAUSE's *discharge sheet from* DEFENSE LAWYER #2.)

KRAUSE: Yeah.

DEFENSE LAWYER #1: Thank you.

DEFENSE LAWYER #2: Mister Krause, you have given depositions and testimony to the Bell family lawyers in this lawsuit case. Is that correct?

KRAUSE: That's correct.

DEFENSE LAWYER #2: But then later there was an attempt to make you a defendant in this case?

KRAUSE: Yeah.

DEFENSE LAWYER #2: What did you think when that happened?

KRAUSE: What did I think? I thought they were a bunch of horses asses. Which I still think today because they are now telling me I'm hostile. You know. I have agreed to do anything they've asked me to do. I drew pictures for them and everything else. And now I'm public enemy number one against the black community, the Bell family, and the attorneys. Well, I have no justification of being hostile to anybody. I'm not here for any reason to stick up for the City, the County or the Bell family. I just want the truth to come out. And the sooner the better.

(KRAUSE *looks pointedly at* PLAINTIFF LAWYER #1.)

DEFENSE LAWYER #2: Mister Krause...

KRAUSE: And another thing. I've been under federal subpoena because of your antics since March 1, 1980. I wish you'd get your act together. We are not practicing law, we are playing games.

DEFENSE LAWYER #2: Mister Krause...

KRAUSE: I mean I have been unemployed because of the publicity on this case since the tenth of March of 1980. It's now '81. It's eighteen, nineteen months. I have now found employment and now I'm tied up with the Daniel Bell case some more.

PLAINTIFF LAWYER #1: Well, you do want the truth to come out, don't you? Didn't you just get finished saying that?

DEFENSE LAWYER #2: This is my examination, counsel!

PLAINTIFF LAWYER #1: Then ask him a question!

(General hubbub, all LAWYERS *at once.)*

DEFENSE LAWYER #1: There is no need to...

DEFENSE LAWYER #2: I will if you'd...

PLAINTIFF LAWYER #1: Instead of just letting him make speeches.

KRAUSE: I've got a right to...

SYLVIA: Mister Krause.

*(*LAWYERS *freeze.)*

KRAUSE: What?

SYLVIA: Have you even been convicted of committing a crime?

KRAUSE: Yes.

SYLVIA: When was the last time you were found guilty of committing a crime?

KRAUSE: February of this year, I believe it was.

*(*LAWYERS *come to life again.)*

DEFENSE LAWYER #1: And that was for issuing worthless checks?

KRAUSE: That's correct.

DEFENSE LAWYER #1: And involved about six thousand dollars worth of checks.

KRAUSE: A little more than that.

DEFENSE LAWYER #1: And you were also found guilty of passing worthless checks in December of 1980? Is that right?

KRAUSE: That was all part of the same thing I'm pretty sure.

DEFENSE LAWYER #1: I see. Weren't you also found guilty of passing worthless checks in April of '76?

KRAUSE: Yes.

DEFENSE LAWYER #1: And in February of '76 you were found guilty of theft by fraud?

KRAUSE: Yes.

DEFENSE LAWYER #1: And in September of '74, issuing worthless checks?

KRAUSE: I believe so.

DEFENSE LAWYER #1: January of '71, issuing worthless checks?

KRAUSE: It's possible.

DEFENSE LAWYER #1: In May of '67, issuing worthless checks?

KRAUSE: I guess so. If you know. You've got my record there. You know. I don't know.

DEFENSE LAWYER #1: There is no reason to believe this is wrong.

KRAUSE: No. I'm not disagreeing with you a bit.

DEFENSE LAWYER #1: In 1959, issuing worthless...

KRAUSE: Look. I wrote those checks because it was the only way I could survive, okay? Besides, why should I obey the law when the Milwaukee Detective Bureau didn't obey the goddam law in 1958, all right?

DEFENSE LAWYER #1: That's a matter of opinion.

KRAUSE: That's a fact.

DEFENSE LAWYER #1: But just an opinion.

KRAUSE: Just an opinion? It is a fact.

DEFENSE LAWYER #1: I am not going to argue with you. You have no right to ask questions.

KRAUSE: I can't ask questions?

DEFENSE LAWYER #1: No, you can't.

KRAUSE: Oh, okay. That's one-sided. Is that what you're saying?

DEFENSE LAWYER #1: That's what a lawsuit is.

KRAUSE: Okay, it's one-sided. I don't get a chance to defend myself. Is that what you're saying? Then there's no...

DEFENSE LAWYER #1: You're not accused of anything that I know of.

KRAUSE: You're damned right.

DEFENSE LAWYER #1: Except conflicting testimony.

KRAUSE: Now look...

DEFENSE LAWYER #2: Mister Krause. Did you have a nickname while you were on the Police Department?

KRAUSE: What? Yeah. I guess I did.

DEFENSE LAWYER #2: What was that nickname?

KRAUSE: Squirrel, I think.

DEFENSE LAWYER #2: Do you know how that nickname developed?

KRAUSE: No.

DEFENSE LAWYER #2: Squirrel was your nickname.

KRAUSE: I think that's what it was.

DEFENSE LAWYER #2: Do you know if it had anything to do with what squirrels collect for the winter?

KRAUSE: I don't think it was meant in that...in a derogatory manner, and I don't think that has any bearing on this case. My character is not on trial here.

DEFENSE LAWYER #2: We know that, Mister Krause.

KRAUSE: *(Standing and shouting)* Well, I'm repeating it just the same. My character is not on trial!

(KRAUSE exits. Court action freezes.)

SYLVIA: Trial? Yes, indeed. Part of a trial, that was.

(PROSPECTIVE JURORS enter. Ten different jurors all played by a white man, white woman, black man, black woman. Changes made by having actors add or subtract an article of clothing to change character.)

SYLVIA: 'Cause on October 3, 1979, my brother Patrick, a special administrator of Dan's estate and representing our entire family, asked for damages against the City of Milwaukee of twenty-five million compensatory and seventy-five million punitive. The lawsuit trial was held in United States District Court, Eastern District of Wisconsin. The opening remarks of the trial were made October 15, 1981. And I was...

PLAINTIFF LAWYER #1: *(To WHITE MAN #1)* Have you ever heard people use the term nigger?

(SYLVIA, taken by surprise, remembers.)

WHITE MAN #1: Yes.

SYLVIA: No, wait.

PLAINTIFF LAWYER #1: Have you ever used the term nigger yourself?

SYLVIA: First they had to pick a jury.

WHITE MAN #1: Probably like jokingly, but I can't say I've ever directed it at a black person as a derogatory remark or anything.

SYLVIA: Seven days to pick a jury.

(Each JUROR *is isolated by light during questioning.)*

PLAINTIFF LAWYER #1: Can you tell us about the instances where you or another have used the word nigger with reference to black people?

WHITE MAN #1: I suppose in athletics or something, where they talk about somebody, some of the professional athletes. That type of thing.

PLAINTIFF LAWYER #1: Do you feel that's unfair to black people?

WHITE MAN #1: I don't really know how to answer that because like I never really had that much contact with black people. I don't know if all of them feel that that term is a real bad remark towards them. I just don't know how I can really answer that.

PLAINTIFF LAWYER #2: *(To* WHITE WOMAN #1*)* In terms of, let's say, your overhearing a customer in one of your restaurants use the term nigger to describe black people, how does that make you feel?

WHITE WOMAN #1: I think that's in bad taste. Although it would depend how they would use it. I've heard blacks call one another nigger, but I mean I know these people are friends and they are not offended by it. But I myself, I wouldn't care to hear someone mention it to me that way.

PLAINTIFF LAWYER #1: *(To* WHITE MAN #1*)* What does the phrase racial discrimination mean to you?

WHITE MAN #1: Unequal treatment for equal people.

PLAINTIFF LAWYER #1: Have you personally experienced any instance o unequal treatment for equal people?

WHITE MAN #1: No.

PLAINTIFF LAWYER #1: Have you ever had an experience which left you with any bad feeling with respect to any black person?

WHITE MAN #1: No.

PLAINTIFF LAWYER #1: Do you think black people are treated unfairly in employment, housing, law enforcement, the courts?

WHITE MAN #1: Well, it seems like more of them are unemployed than white people. I don't know actually what the real problem is there. But that's all I can say on it.

(PLAINTIFF LAWYER #2 and DEFENSE LAWYER #2 speak simultaneously to WHITE WOMAN #1 and BLACK WOMAN respectively.)

LAWYERS: What high school did you go to?

WHITE WOMAN #1: Polaski.

BLACK WOMAN: Rufus King.

LAWYERS: Was it integrated?

WHITE WOMAN #1: No.

BLACK WOMAN: Yes.

PLAINTIFF LAWYER #2: All white?

DEFENSE LAWYER #2: Primarily white?

WHITE WOMAN #1: Yes.

BLACK WOMAN: About half and half.

PLAINTIFF LAWYER #2: And your junior high school?

WHITE WOMAN #1: Audubon.

PLAINTIFF LAWYER #2: Integrated then?

WHITE WOMAN #1: No.

PLAINTIFF LAWYER #2: Grade school?

WHITE WOMAN #1: All white.

DEFENSE LAWYER #2: Now when you were going to that high school were you living in an integrated neighborhood?

BLACK WOMAN: Yes. There was still whites in the neighborhood.

DEFENSE LAWYER #2: Did you have any friends that were other than black people while you were in high school?

BLACK WOMAN: Yes.

DEFENSE LAWYER #2: Have you kept up contacts with those people?

BLACK WOMAN: No.

DEFENSE LAWYER #2: Where you live now, is that an integrated neighborhood?

BLACK WOMAN: I'd say it's ninety-eight percent black.

DEFENSE LAWYER #2: And you've said that you've always lived in the inner city?

BLACK WOMAN: Yes.

DEFENSE LAWYER #2: What do you mean by that?

BLACK WOMAN: I guess it's an area where concentration is more black than white.

DEFENSE LAWYER #2: I assume because you moved around within that area that you prefer to stay in that neighborhood, is that correct?

BLACK WOMAN: I can't afford to go anywhere else.

PLAINTIFF LAWYER #2: *(To* WHITE MAN #2) Sir, where you live, is that an integrated neighborhood?

WHITE MAN #2: Yes, sir. Our next door neighbors are black.

PLAINTIFF LAWYER #2: And are you more friendly, less friendly with that neighbor than other people in your immediate neighborhood?

WHITE MAN #2: No. We are all very friendly.

PLAINTIFF LAWYER #1: *(To* WHITE WOMAN #2*)* In terms of your feelings about blacks in Milwaukee when you left in 1979, how did that enter into your decision to go to West Bend?

WHITE WOMAN #2: Well, I feel a lot safer out there. I enjoy the country out there. And I'm very glad to be out of Milwaukee.

PLAINTIFF LAWYER #1: Do you have much contacts with blacks in West Bend?

WHITE WOMAN #2: Oh, I don't know if I've ever seen a black person in West Bend. I might have seen one, but it's a white community.

PLAINTIFF LAWYER #2: *(To* WHITE MAN #3*)* Sir, about how many years as your neighborhood been integrated?

WHITE MAN #3: Well, we moved in in 1973. And, well, it varies. Now our block hasn't got hardly any, and then further over it's quite a few. It varies.

PLAINTIFF LAWYER #2: Was it somewhat integrated in 1973?

WHITE MAN #3: Yes, it was. Not quite as bad...I shouldn't say bad. That's a bad thing to say. I mean there weren't as many as there are now. But I have no problem with anybody.

PLAINTIFF LAWYER #1: *(To* WHITE WOMAN #3*)* Have you ever witnessed or even heard about racial discrimination or racial prejudice?

WHITE WOMAN #3: Not that I'm aware of.

PLAINTIFF LAWYER #1: Have you ever had any unfortunate experience with a situation where you thought a person was acting as a racist?

WHITE WOMAN #3: No.

PLAINTIFF LAWYER #1: Have you had any personal conversations with black people—let's say, in the last ten years—other than like, let's say, a sales person?

WHITE WOMAN #3: Nothing I can remember.

PLAINTIFF LAWYER #2: *(To* WHITE MAN #4*)* Sir, is your neighborhood integrated?

WHITE MAN #4: Oh, yeah. It's comin'.

PLAINTIFF LAWYER #2: It's coming or it's already...

WHITE MAN #4: It's already there.

PLAINTIFF LAWYER #2: And what is your closest black neighbor?

WHITE MAN #4: Two doors.

PLAINTIFF LAWYER #2: Two doors away. And about how many black neighbors are there on your block?

WHITE MAN #4: Well, just that. The one two doors south of me. That's it.

PLAINTIFF LAWYER #2: Are you at all friendly with them? Do you have a chance to chat with them or anything?

WHITE MAN #4: We stay in our yard. They stay in their yard.

DEFENSE LAWYER #2: *(To* BLACK MAN*)* Sir, you said that you remembered the shooting of Daniel Bell, although you were fairly young when it happened?

BLACK MAN: Right.

DEFENSE LAWYER #2: What did you think about the incident at that time?

BLACK MAN: I was upset. I was real upset.

DEFENSE LAWYER #2: Why were you upset?

BLACK MAN: Because I didn't think the police gave him a fair chance.

DEFENSE LAWYER #2: Did you think at the time that racism had something to do with the shooting?

BLACK MAN: I think very much so it had something to do with it.

DEFENSE LAWYER #2: Do you still think it did?

BLACK MAN: I think it did.

PLAINTIFF LAWYER #2: *(To* WHITE WOMAN #4*)* Do you think that the principle of affirmative action rests on compensation for past discrimination?

WHITE WOMAN #4: We can't compensate for what we haven't done for years.

SYLVIA: Can't compensate?

(All leave the stage except SYLVIA *and* WHITE WOMAN #4*.)*

WHITE WOMAN #4: No. We can't do it all at one time.

SYLVIA: Let me tell you something about Dan.

WHITE WOMAN #4: I think that's my objection.

SYLVIA: A couple of weeks before he was killed he'd been in jail a few days 'cause he couldn't pay a hundred dollar fine for not havin' a valid driver's license.

WHITE WOMAN #4: You see, it's going to take some time for certain people to catch up.

SYLVIA: And I had bailed him out.

WHITE WOMAN #4: But they've got to make the effort.

SYLVIA: You see, although he could drive real good he couldn't read and write too good.

WHITE WOMAN #4: And I don't like giving something away until the time is right.

SYLVIA: So he had trouble with the written test.

WHITE WOMAN #4: You know what I mean?

SYLVIA: Which made him have to drive without a license.

WHITE WOMAN #4: You don't understand what I'm saying.

(Audio over the rest of the sequence of original chase sounds: running, breathing, etc.)

SYLVIA: And so those polices...

WHITE WOMAN #4: A job is a job.

SYLVIA: They maybe scared him.

WHITE WOMAN #4: It's needed by the blacks, by the whites.

SYLVIA: I don't know.

WHITE WOMAN #4: It's needed by the Spanish equally.

SYLVIA: But it's a helluva thing in this here country—not being able to read good.

WHITE WOMAN #4: Now, I understand...

SYLVIA: Right, Mrs Clark?

WHITE WOMAN #4: the need to bring more minorities...

SYLVIA: A helluva thing.

WHITE WOMAN #4: into the work force at a quicker pace.

SYLVIA: Education, jobs, license, work.

WHITE WOMAN #4: But I don't want to see the white people or those who have been in those jobs for many years pushed aside to elevate somebody who is not ready to be elevated.

SYLVIA: Run, Danny!

(Gunshot. Quick blackout on WHITE WOMAN #4. SYLVIA *alone. Audio of* DOUGLAS *at age seven.)*

DOUGLAS: Mama, they killed Dan!

*(*ERNEST, JIMMY, *and* PATRICK *enter through door in a rush. It is February 2, 1958.)*

PATRICK: Sylvia.

SYLVIA: Oh, my God, my God!

*(*SYLVIA *hugs each of them.)*

PATRICK: Look here. We's goin' down.

ERNEST: Gonna get at the truth.

PATRICK: Detectives come by the house, tried to tell me somethin'.

JIMMY: Somethin' about a knife.

SYLVIA: I know. The T V say...

PATRICK: So we's all goin' down.

SYLVIA: But it don't make no sense.

JIMMY: None of it do.

SYLVIA: 'Cause look.

(Getting DAN'*s knife. They all look at it in her hand.)*

PATRICK: Why, that's...

SYLVIA: Danny's. Yes.

ERNEST: Dammit.

(Slight pause)

PATRICK: They'll want...they'll want us to identify the body.

SYLVIA: No, no. I couldn't.

PATRICK: That's all right, sis. Jimmy, Ernest'll do it.

JIMMY: Yeah. We see to it.

(PATRICK *gets* SYLVIA'*s winter coat and holds it open for her.*)

PATRICK: Gotta be done, sis.

SYLVIA: My God.

(SYLVIA *puts on the coat.*)

ERNEST: Let's go, okay?

(*All exit.* POLICE SERGEANT *appears at desk remaining on stage from trial scene.* PATRICK *and* SYLVIA *rush in from another stage area.*)

PATRICK: We Daniel Bell's kin and—

SYLVIA: We wanna know...

POLICE SERGEANT: Now, wait.

SYLVIA: What happened?

POLICE SERGEANT: Wait.

PATRICK: How could he...

SYLVIA: Why?

PATRICK: Those detectives, they say...

SYLVIA: And on the T V...

PATRICK: What'd my brother do?

POLICE SERGEANT: It was self-defense, self-defense, all right? So just calm down. Officer was just trying to protect himself, that's all.

SYLVIA: Why?

POLICE SERGEANT: The kid attacked him, lunged at him with a knife.

SYLVIA: No, uh-uh.

PATRICK: Couldn't have been.

POLICE SERGEANT: Don't you tell me what couldn't have been. Because we've got the officer's statement. And the knife.

SYLVIA: No. *(She brings out* DAN's *knife.)* 'Cause it's here. This is his knife. Right here.

*(*POLICE SERGEANT *is taken aback for a moment.)*

POLICE SERGEANT: Well, then you just give me that knife. Give it here.

SYLVIA: No, I ain't gonna give you nothin' 'cause my brother didn't have a knife tonight.

POLICE SERGEANT: Well, you just...

PATRICK: And even if he did have a knife and he jumped out of the car and such like they say, why didn't the police just shoot him when he jumped out if he was bein' attacked?

POLICE SERGEANT: Were you they? No. Now this is police work. You don't know nothing about it. The officer shot in self-defense.

SYLVIA: In the back?

POLICE SERGEANT: Well...

PATRICK: How can you shoot a man in the back if he cuttin' at you?

POLICE SERGEANT: Look, just get outta here, okay? Can't tell you niggers nothin'.

PATRICK: We...

*(*SYLVIA *restrains* PATRICK.)*

POLICE SERGEANT: Get out, I said! Or I'll throw the both of you in jail!

*(*PATRICK *and* SYLVIA *back away. Lights out on* POLICE SERGEANT. *He exits.* SYLVIA *exits.* PATRICK *alone.)*

PATRICK: It just...it just made my family feel so small. Made me feel small. Little and all like that. And I'm not educated or nothin' like that. But I'm just, just a good plain citizen, been workin' ever since I been in this town, payin' taxes, and all that stuff. And then what did my brother get? A bullet in the back.

(PATRICK exits. JIMMY and ERNEST enter. MORGUE ATTENDANT pushes a gurney onto the stage. DAN is on the gurney with a sheet over him. MORGUE ATTENDANT raises the sheet.)

MORGUE ATTENDANT: This him?

(JIMMY and ERNEST look at the body. ERNEST turns away quickly. JIMMY just keeps staring.)

ERNEST: I was home lyin' in my bed and an ambulance passed by with my brother in it one night about 9:30, somethin' like that, about 9:30.

MORGUE ATTENDANT: *(To JIMMY)* Well, is it?

(JIMMY nods. MORGUE ATTENDANT takes out a form and a pen.)

MORGUE ATTENDANT: You've got to sign this form then.

(JIMMY just looks at the form.)

MORGUE ATTENDANT: Sign it, please.

(JIMMY signs the form. MORGUE ATTENDANT exits with the form. JIMMY stands frozen, staring at the sheet covering the body.)

ERNEST: The next day I didn't go to work, see, because I was slaughterin', workin' in the hide department at Patrick Cudahy, in the head department, bustin', cuttin' meat. And I didn't go to work that Monday mornin' 'cause I didn't know if Dan had any insurance or anything so the credit union didn't open until Tuesday and I went back to work that Tuesday and put in for about six hundred dollars to take his body down South. That is about fifteen hundred miles from here, altogether it's around thirty hundred miles, so we drove three cars down to the funeral, about eighteen of us went down there.

(*Baptist church music comes up and* PATRICK *re-enters.*)

PATRICK: Now, the funeral...the funeral at Galilee Baptist Church in Springfield, well, I'm going to say it was sad. And the ushers was standin' one after another. It was such a deep grief until you know, they who was just participatin', they just went out, fell out. My father, he just fell out. Had to take out three or four of them, the brothers. It was just an awful thing, extraordinary confusion in the heart and mind.

(SYLVIA *re-enters. She approaches* JIMMY.)

SYLVIA: Jimmy.

(JIMMY *looks at the sheet.*)

SYLVIA: Jimmy?

(JIMMY *continues to stare at the sheet. He makes a movement toward the sheet, then slowly, then hurriedly exits—in silence.*)

SYLVIA: Jimmy!

(SYLVIA *looks at* ERNEST.)

SYLVIA: Jimmy and Ernest...well, they sorta cracked up, sorta...sorta went out behind Dan's death. Maybe because...

ERNEST: (*Smiling*) My mother had triplets, you know, three, six, nine, twelve boys, and one girl. I thought she had triplets, had born three at one time. Jimmy, Dan, and I was together.

SYLVIA: They was so close.

ERNEST: The three of us together. And Henry, Pat and
Eddie was together. And Joe, Speedy and Dolphus
was together. And Roosevelt, Walter and Alphonzo.
Triplets. And that took effect on me. Then later I got
feelin' on my job, couldn't take it no longer up on the
assembly line. It seemed like they was killin' peoples
out there. I seen all that blood and stuff and I started
callin' names and didn't know what I was doin'. Some
of the white sisters was out there sayin' I was their
blood brother an all like that, so two nurses came and
got me off the assembly line and brought me to the first
aid and they took my arm and told my sister—told my
brother Patrick and my sister—that I had quit my job,
and I went in the hospital that night and I stayed in the
hospital about fourteen or fifteen years in the hospital
in different other hospitals about fifteen years. Then
they pulled all my teeth out and...well, I was no more
good.

SYLVIA: Jimmy's still in the hospital now. 'Cause he
can't do for hisself too good on the outside. And
Ernest...well, he...

ERNEST: *(Wide-eyed)* I seen the knife, though. I seen the
knife he had. I seen where they pull the knife out of the
hand there. I seen that on T V. And I believe it. I think
the T V don't lie. But I seen where they pulled the knife
out of him, stuck it up in his heart like that, pulled it
out of him. *(Agitated)* I seen that on T V, the knife. It
was green, green stuff come out of him, the cop pulled
the knife out of him. I work with a lot of knives, I have
worked with knives for about nine and a half years,
nothin' but knives, all kinds of knives, trick knives
where they split them heads wide open and take the
brains out and all kind of different types of meat they
take off when they get through. We was killin' eight,
nine hundred an hour. *(Very distraught)* When Dan got
killed I took his picture out there to the slaughterhouse

the next mornin' and showed it to my foreman and
all the peoples in the department, I showed them the
picture so I got two weeks off from work, they give me
two weeks off for my vacation because me and Dan
and Jimmy was fixin' to go down South in a brand new
car, I was goin' to buy a brand new car, but my brother
bought the brand new car so I couldn't...

(SYLVIA *catches* ERNEST *as he breaks down sobbing. Long
pause as* SYLVIA *holds him up, holds him tightly. Tears in
his eyes,* ERNEST *now speaks very softly.*)

ERNEST: Well...I cried all the time. I couldn't hardly
talk. I just cried all the time. They rubbed my back and
all like that...I seen...I know...I seen his body in the
casket...I know he was dead.

(SYLVIA *releases* ERNEST *and he exits slowly.*)

SYLVIA: And so are you too now, Ernest. Dead.

(GRADY *has appeared by the casket.*)

GRADY: Well, we looked at him, and we could tell he
was dead, regrettable as it was.

(SYLVIA *turns to look at* GRADY.)

GRADY: And we were scared and panicked, and I don't
know, in hysteria. And I'm thinking pure preservation,
self-preservation only.

SYLVIA: Preservation...self-preservation... (*She goes to
her dictionary.*) To preserve. To protect. To maintain....
Somethin' I can relate to, Mrs Clark. Somethin' like
what you and Papa taught me.

(VORPAGEL *has entered.*)

VORPAGEL: Grady used to get letters with cash in them
after the shooting.

SYLVIA: But then what about this?

VORPAGEL: There'd be three one-dollar bills from some guy or five bucks from somebody else. He got a half dozen I know of. He once showed me a letter from a "fan". It started to the effect congratulations to a police officer who knows how to do the job. That's the way to take care of niggers. Here is two dollars for more bullets. And Grady's tone of voice was that of being proud of what he had done, bragging about what he had done, and feeling good that the citizens of the City of Milwaukee were giving him support.

(GRADY *exits.*)

VORPAGEL: You see, the temper of the times in 1958 was vastly different from what it is today.

SYLVIA: Different.

(*Courtroom scene comes to life again.* JUDGE *and others enter.*)

DEFENSE LAWYER #1: Now, Mister Vorpagel, during your investigation the night of February 2, 1958, did you check the scene for a knife?

VORPAGEL: I did.

DEFENSE LAWYER #1: And was a knife found?

VORPAGEL: There was no knife at the scene when I arrived.

DEFENSE LAWYER #1: And did you find out why?

VORPAGEL: Yes. Patrolman Randa had picked the knife up out of the snow after it fell out of the deceased's hands according to Patrolman Randa's statement, which I later read.

DEFENSE LAWYER #1: And it fell out of the deceased's hand when they were putting the body on the stretcher, isn't that right?

VORPAGEL: According to his statement, yes.

DEFENSE LAWYER #1: So you knew there was a knife recovered at the scene.

VORPAGEL: I was told.

DEFENSE LAWYER #1: Did you have any reason to believe, when you read the report, that that was untrue?

VORPAGEL: Yes.

DEFENSE LAWYER #1: And what was your reason?

VORPAGEL: I felt that if a man had been slashed at with a knife, that would be the first thing he would tell me. Grady told me he shot Bell because he was a fleeing felon. He said nothing about being slashed at with a knife.

(Scene freezes.)

SYLVIA: The knife, the knife...it cut deep, that cop's knife did...but that...that was just the beginning. Just the spark.

(SYLVIA exits. Scene comes alive again.)

PLAINTIFF LAWYER #1: So you say that there was a meeting held in the District Attorney McCauley's office on the morning of February 3, 1958?

VORPAGEL: Yes.

PLAINTIFF LAWYER #1: Tell us who was there and what happened.

(LAWYERS exit. Entering are: GLASER, GRADY, INSPECTOR SERGEANT SHAFFER, KRAUSE, McCAULEY and WOELFEL. VORPAGEL already in the scene. Everyone is talking at once: arguing, asking questions.)

McCAULEY: All right, wait a minute. Just wait a minute here!

(Everyone falls silent. McCAULEY looks through the reports on his desk. Then he looks up.)

MCCAULEY: All right, Grady. Tell me again. You say you shot in self-defense.

GRADY: Yes, sir. Because Bell lunged at me with a knife.

MCCAULEY: From six feet away.

GRADY: Yes, sir.

MCCAULEY: But Krause's report says that you were ten or fifteen feet away when you fired.

KRAUSE: Well, sir...

MCCAULEY: Just hold it a minute, Krause.

KRAUSE: Yes, sir.

MCCAULEY: And Detective Vorpagel, you say that you and Detective Hughes measure twenty-three feet nine inches from some block of ice.

VORPAGEL: Yes, sir. As our diagram indicates.

MCCAULEY: And this is where you say Grady told you he fired from last night?

VORPAGEL: Yes, sir.

GRADY: No, sir, that's not what I said.

KRAUSE: I don't think that...

MCCAULEY: Wait a minute, dammit! Look. These reports aren't consistent. I can't do anything with them!

(Pause. MCCAULEY calls WOELFEL over to him.)

MCCAULEY: Woelfel.

(They converse in private. MCCAULEY then goes back to his desk.)

WOELFEL: *(Calling)* Vorpagel.

(VORPAGEL goes over to WOELFEL.)

WOELFEL:Your report isn't consistent, Vorpagel. I want you to change it to include the fact that Officer Grady shot Bell because Bell slashed at him with a knife.

VORPAGEL: But...

WOELFEL: Not just because Bell was a fleeing felon.

VORPAGEL: But this is the first I'm...

WOELFEL: And...

VORPAGEL: Hearing this.

WOELFEL: And your diagram isn't really correct so you should just get rid of the damn thing.

VORPAGEL: I can't, sir.

WOELFEL: Can't what? Change your report or get rid of the diagram?

VORPAGEL: Both. (*Pause*) Okay. But you're going to have to speak to Inspector Glaser about this.

(WOELFEL *goes over to* GLASER *and speaks to him privately.* WOELFEL *hands him the questioned papers, then goes over to where* MCCAULEY *and the others are.* GLASER *motions for* VORPAGEL. VORPAGEL *comes over.*)

GLASER: Listen, Vorpagel, we've got a problem here. A little consistency is all we're after. Nothing major. Okay? So just do everybody a favor and change your report. The Bell kid slashed at Grady with a knife. That's why he shot. You heard him say that. I mean, after all, he was there.

VORPAGEL: I can't do that.

GLASER: Why not?

VORPAGEL: That's not what he said to me last night.

GLASER: Come on, Vorpagel. So he left out a couple of details in the heat of it all? Why sweat it? Just change the report and get rid of the diagram.

VORPAGEL:No.

(Everyone just looks at VORPAGEL *for a moment. Then all eyes train on* MCCAULEY. *He picks up the reports from* GLASER *and waves them around.)*

MCCAULEY: Well, I'll say it again. These damn things have got to be consistent! *(He looks at* VORPAGEL.*)* I want you to change your report.

VORPAGEL: I can't do that, sir.

MCCAULEY: I said change it.

VORPAGEL: No, sir.

MCCAULEY: Change it, dammit!

VORPAGEL: No! I've written things down the way they were told to me at the scene last night.

(Courtroom scene people enter as MCCAULEY *office scene people exit.)*

PLAINTIFF LAWYER #1: What did you do then?

VORPAGEL: I left.

PLAINTIFF LAWYER #1: And do you know what happened in that room after you left?

DEFENSE LAWYER #1: Objection. Calls for hearsay.

PLAINTIFF LAWYER #1: I withdraw the question.

DEFENSE LAWYER #1: So you're saying you were ordered to change your report?

VORPAGEL: Yes, counsel.

DEFENSE LAWYER #1: But after this, you were never disciplined for disobeying any order, were you?

VORPAGEL: No, I was not.

DEFENSE LAWYER #1: Now, when you were ordered, as you say, to change your report, if that was done with the intent that you make a false report, it would have been in violation of the criminal statute of the State of

Wisconsin which prohibited a person from obstructing justice. Would it not?

VORPAGEL: At that time I knew of no statute that dealt with obstruction of justice, counsel, so I can't answer that question.

DEFENSE LAWYER #1: Well, you went to law school. Wouldn't you say that that would be a criminal act?

PLAINTIFF LAWYER #1: Objection.

JUDGE: Sustained.

DEFENSE LAWYER #1: Well, when you went to law school at Marquette, did you study criminal law?

PLAINTIFF LAWYER #1: Objection, your Honor.

JUDGE: Sustained. He said he didn't know.

(Lights change to indicate the passage of time.)

DEFENSE LAWYER #1: Did you tell them you were not going to put the knife-slashing in your report because you didn't believe it?

VORPAGEL: No.

DEFENSE LAWYER #1: Why not?

VORPAGEL: I thought it was unnecessary.

DEFENSE LAWYER #1: You felt it was unnecessary that the investigating detective doesn't believe a version of the story, not to tell that to the District Attorney?

PLAINTIFF LAWYER #1: Objection, argumentation.

JUDGE: Overruled.

VORPAGEL: As an office working the particular case, everything that was told to me was hearsay. I was putting down the things that were told to me. And as an office you form certain opinions. And by the time I got through sitting there in Mister McCauley's office, it was very, very firm in my mind that there was something fishy in the case. I didn't think that they were telling the truth, but I had no way of proving it at the time. I was hearing different stories from the first time. But I didn't feel that it was my job to directly accuse a man of lying until I had further information.

PLAINTIFF LAWYER #1: Now do you have an opinion as to whether these individuals, McCauley, Glaser, Woelfel, Shaffer, Grady, and Krause, whether they were acting individually or acting in concert? Did you have an opinion?

VORPAGEL: Did I have...

DEFENSE LAWYER #1: Objection. It's irrelevant.

JUDGE: Overruled.

VORPAGEL: I did have an opinion, yes.

DEFENSE LAWYER #1: Also no foundation.

PLAINTIFF LAWYER #1: What is that opinion?

DEFENSE LAWYER #1: Objecting on the basis of foundation, your Honor.

JUDGE: Well, he was there. I think the foundation...he's giving his views, what happened, what his perception was at this meeting. Objection overruled.

PLAINTIFF LAWYER #1: What is your opinion?

VORPAGEL: My opinion is they were acting in concert.

PLAINTIFF LAWYER #1: In concert.

VORPAGEL: Yes.

(JUDGE *strikes gavel. All except* SYLVIA *leave.* VORPAGEL *is last to leave and* SYLVIA *stops him.*)

SYLVIA: Mr. Vorpagel.

VORPAGEL: Yes.

SYLVIA: Why? Why did you just walk away back then, abandon us?

VORPAGEL: I didn't just...

SYLVIA: You did.

VORPAGEL: But you see...

SYLVIA: You put yourself through college, joined the
F B I, moved on up in the ranks. You could at least
have told somebody there.

VORPAGEL: You've got to understand.

SYLVIA: I'm tryin' to.

VORPAGEL: When you become a police officer, one of
the first things you learn is to take the facts as you see
them and are given them and present them in court or
present them to a District Attorney or a city attorney.
if you think a violation has taken place, you take your
information in, you apply for a warrant. If a warrant
is issued, you go to court and the case is tried. You tell
the best you can. And if you lose, for whatever reason,
you are taught not to take the case with you. You don't
harbor on it, dwell on it. When you do not have the
decision that you wish, that's the decision, nonetheless,
and you're stuck with it. There's nothing you can do
once a case has gone to court. That's it. It's over.

SYLVIA: Just like that?

(VORPAGEL *says nothing.*)

SYLVIA: Just like that?!

VORPAGEL: There was nothing I could do! (*Pause. He
softens his voice.*) Even my minister told me that there
was nothing I could do.

SYLVIA: Even your minister?

(VORPAGEL *turns away from* SYLVIA *and exits.*)

SYLVIA: Words. Words. (*She goes to her desk—her papers,
transcripts, etc.*) Hundreds, thousands of pages of
words. A mountain of 'em. Heroes, villains, charges,

counter-charges, apologies, excuses! *Words!* I like to drown in 'em, Mrs Clark. They like to drag me down. Too much said. Not enough done. And all I could picture at times was Danny lyin' there. Cold and dead. A picture with no caption, no words. And I wanted to leap up in that courtroom. Leap to my feet and shake my dictionary in they faces. I wanted to shout to all of 'em: No! Please, no more. No more words. No more but one. Just one! Just...

(Lights come up quickly on JUDGE.*)*

JUDGE: Ladies and gentlemen. Let it be known that the seven-member jury in the Daniel Bell case, Civil Action No. 79-C927, has found this day, Wednesday, December 16, 1981, that there was a conspiracy to cover up the truth about his death and that race was a factor in said conspiracy.

SYLVIA: Danny? Papa? Everybody? Did you hear? Did you hear that?

JUDGE: Let it also be known that his family is herewith awarded in excess of a million dollars.

(Blackout on JUDGE. *Simultaneously, a series of* VOICES *begin speaking and then shouting at* SYLVIA *from the shadows. They steadily increase in intensity until all the* VOICES *are screaming at once.)*

VOICE #1: A million dollars?

VOICE #2: Did he say a million dollars?

VOICE #3: Not a million dollars.

VOICE #4: A million dollars for what?

VOICE #5: Yeah, that's what I'd like to know.

VOICE #6: Me, too.

VOICE #1: You were only in it for the money.

VOICE #2: That Bell kid, he was nothing but a troublemaker anyway.

VOICE #3: They took the city, that's what they did.

VOICE #4: Should of stayed down on the farm in Louisiana, that's what they should of done.

VOICE #5: Why'd he run anyway? He shouldn't have run. Never run from the police, from authority.

VOICE #6: What's past is past. They should have been satisfied with a few dollars out of court.

SYLVIA: NO!

(VOICES *fall silent.*)

SYLVIA: 'Cause we was right. Right. Even the United States Court of Appeals finally said so three years later. We got a real, uncontested verdict then. Not the money! *(Pause)* Justice. *(She walks back to her desk and looks at all the books and documents.)* Well, Mrs Clark, I've read through it all, studied over it, worked my way into and out of it, 'cause I figured that if I did I'd be able to come to some sorta conclusion. But I haven't. 'Cause it's sorta endless. Endless. Just like education itself, I guess. Education. The least of what I—we— want. Right here. In our own country. America. 'Cause it's about education. *(Pause)* Right, Mrs Clark? *(Pause)* Right, Sylvia.

(Lights fade to black.)

END OF PLAY